Marlies Glasius • Meta de Lange
Jos Bartman • Emanuela Dalmasso
Aofei Lv • Adele Del Sordi
Marcus Michaelsen • Kris Ruijgrok

Research, Ethics and Risk in the Authoritarian Field

Marlies Glasius
Meta de Lange
Jos Bartman
Emanuela Dalmasso
Aofei Lv
Adele Del Sordi
Marcus Michaelsen
Kris Ruijgrok
University of Amsterdam
Amsterdam, The Netherlands

The research leading to these results has received funding from the European Research Council (FP7/2007-2013) / ERC grant agreement n° 323899.

https://doi.org/10.1007/978-3-319-68966-1

To everyone who has helped us in the authoritarian field, and especially to those who have remained anonymous. Without them, field research would be impossible.

Contents

About the Authors

Jos Bartman is a PhD candidate at the Department of Politics, University of Amsterdam, and a team member of *Authoritarianism in a Global Age*. His research focuses on how subnational authoritarian regimes use repression. During his research master's, he conducted four months of fieldwork in rural West Bengal (India). For his current research, he has conducted fieldwork in Veracruz (Mexico) and Gujarat (India), where he has interviewed targets and executors of political repression.

Emanuela Dalmasso is a post-doctoral researcher at the Department of Politics, University of Amsterdam, for the research project *Authoritarianism in a Global Age*. She holds a PhD in political science from the University of Turin (Italy). Her main areas of expertise and interest are Middle Eastern politics and gender studies, with a specific focus on Morocco. She has previously published on these topics in the *Journal of Modern African Studies*, *Totalitarian Movements and Political Religions*, *Contemporary Arab Affairs*, and *Mediterranean Politics*. Her work is based on extensive fieldwork in Morocco and Tunisia.

Meta de Lange is a junior researcher at the Department of Politics, University of Amsterdam, where she contributes to the project *Authoritarianism in a Global Age* with organizational and research support. She graduated from the Political Science Department at the University of Amsterdam in 2012 with a master's thesis based on interviews with Occupy activists in Amsterdam. She gained fieldwork experience in Surinam (2005), interviewing youths in detention, and in Cameroon (2006) conducting interviews on the impact of HIV/AIDS in a rural area.

Adele Del Sordi is a former post-doctoral researcher at the Department of Politics, University of Amsterdam, where she contributed to the project *Authoritarianism in a Global Age* by looking at the impact of globalization on authoritarian sustainability in post-Soviet Kazakhstan. Since November 2017 she has joined the Graduate School of East and South-East European Studies at the University Ludwig-Maximilian in Munich, Germany. She holds a PhD in political systems and institutional change from the Institute of Advanced Studies (IMT) in Lucca, Italy. Her research interests include the stability of authoritarian regimes, post-Soviet politics, and authoritarian learning. She has conducted extensive fieldwork in Kazakhstan between 2011 and 2017.

Marlies Glasius is a professor of international relations at the Department of Politics, University of Amsterdam, and principal investigator of the ERC-funded project *Authoritarianism in a Global Age*. Her research interests include authoritarianism, international criminal justice, human security, and global civil society. She holds a PhD cum laude from the Netherlands School of Human Rights Research and previously worked at the London School of Economics and Political Science (LSE). She is the author of *The International Criminal Court: A Global Civil Society Achievement* (2006) and *Foreign Policy on Human Rights: Its Influence on Indonesia under Soeharto* (1999) and coeditor of volumes on international criminal justice (with Zarkov 2014), on human security (with Kaldor 2006), and on civil society (with Kostovicova 2011, with Lewis and Seckinelgin 2004, and the annual *Global Civil Society* Yearbook, 2001–2011). She has conducted fieldwork in the Central African Republic, Egypt, Greece, Indonesia, Liberia, and Sri Lanka.

Aofei Lv is a post-doctoral researcher at the Department of Politics, University of Amsterdam, for the research project *Authoritarianism in a Global Age*. She finished her PhD at the Politics Department, University of Glasgow, in 2015. She got her bachelor's and master's degree at Nankai University, China. She has conducted fieldwork in China since 2010, including interviews with officials of different departments within the central government, journalists, scholars, senior managers of enterprises, and representatives of international organizations in China.

Marcus Michaelsen is a post-doctoral researcher at the Department of Politics, University of Amsterdam, and a team member of the project *Authoritarianism in a Global Age*. He obtained his PhD in media and communication studies from the University of Erfurt (Germany) with a dissertation on the role of the Internet in Iran's political transformation. He holds a master's degree in Middle Eastern Studies from the Université de Provence (France) and was a research fellow at the Institut Français de Recherche en Iran (IFRI) in Tehran from 2004 to 2006. His research interests include media and political change, digital media activism, and the politics of Internet governance, with a particular focus on Iran and the Middle East. He has conducted fieldwork in Iran and Pakistan.

Kris Ruijgrok is a PhD candidate for the research project *Authoritarianism in a Global Age* at the Department of Politics, University of Amsterdam. His PhD research uses a mixed-methods approach to study the role of Internet in street protests in authoritarian regimes. He holds a cum laude master's degree in political science from the University of Amsterdam. He has recently conducted fieldwork in Malaysia.

List of Abbreviations

CESS	The Central Eurasian Studies Society
DA-RT	Data Access and Research Transparency
DEA	US Drug Enforcement Agency
EU	European Union
EOSC	European Open Science Cloud
ERC	European Research Council
HINDRAF	Hindu Rights Action Force
HIVOS	Humanistisch Instituut voor Ontwikkelingssamenwerking
JETS	Journal Editors' Transparency Statement
NGO	Non-governmental Organization
OSCE	Organization for Security and Co-operation in Europe

CHAPTER 1

Introduction

Abstract In this introduction to *Research, Ethics and Risk in the Authoritarian Field*, we explain why and how we wrote this book, who we are, what the 'authoritarian field' means for us, and who may find this book useful. By recording our joint experiences in very different authoritarian contexts systematically and succinctly, comparing and contrasting them, and drawing lessons, we aim to give other researchers a framework, so they will not need to start from scratch as we did. It is not the absence of free and fair elections, or repression, that most prominently affects our fieldwork in authoritarian contexts, but the arbitrariness of authoritarian rule, and the uncertainty it results in for us and the people in our fieldwork environment.

Keywords Authoritarianism • Field research • Reflection • Uncertainty • Qualitative research • Fieldwork methods

Why This Book

We wrote this book, in the first place, because we needed it and it did not exist. In 2014 we came to the discovery, as a comparative research group preparing for fieldwork, that there was practically no written guidance on how to handle the challenges of authoritarianism research. There were reams of literature on anthropological fieldwork, and some good texts on

M. Glasius et al., *Research, Ethics and Risk in the Authoritarian Field*,
https://doi.org/10.1007/978-3-319-68966-1_1

how to do research on political violence in conflict areas (for instance, Sriram et al. 2009; Mazurana et al. 2013; Hilhorst et al. 2016). But the image they painted of their field did not mirror our experience, and the advice they gave was only partially applicable. Country-based texts were also an imperfect fit: we found some interesting discussion on navigating the party-state in China (Heimer and Thøgersen 2006), or on circumventing the prohibition on mentioning ethnicity in Rwanda (Thomson et al. 2013), but the extensive reflections on Chinese language and culture, or on what it means to be a white researcher in the African Great Lakes region, did not travel. Fortunately, more explicit reflection on research in authoritarian contexts per se is just beginning to emerge. In recent years, two special issues have appeared on 'closed' and 'authoritarian' contexts, respectively (Koch 2013; Goode and Ahram 2016), as well as some shorter pieces focusing on fieldwork challenges in China (Shih 2015), the Middle East (Lynch 2016), and Central Asia (Driscoll 2015), explicitly approached as authoritarian contexts. We have learned from, and draw on, this recent literature. But it still consists largely of collections of individual experiences, placed side by side rather than in conversation with each other. By recording our joint experiences in very different authoritarian contexts systematically and succinctly, comparing and contrasting them, and drawing lessons, we aim to give other researchers a framework, so they will not need to start from scratch as we did.

A second trigger for writing the book was the death of Giulio Regeni. Regeni was a PhD student at the University of Cambridge, who was tortured to death while doing fieldwork on trade unionism in Egypt, in early 2016. Regeni's killing sent shockwaves through the community of Middle East scholars, reminding us of the risk involved in research in the authoritarian field. It affected us quite personally, because some of us knew people close to him, one of us had done research in Egypt only few years earlier, and others were PhD students about to embark on their own fieldwork. At the same time, Regeni's death and the responses to it also highlighted the rarity of such an extreme act of repression against a foreign scholar, and reminded us of our relative safety in comparison to our respondents and collaborators in the countries we study.

A final consideration for writing this book was the controversy that arose among political scientists, primarily in the United States, around the so-called Data Access and Research Transparency (DA-RT) statement. DA-RT asserted that 'researchers should provide access to … data or explain why they cannot', and led to the adoption of a joint transparency statement by a number of journal editors in 2014 (https://www.dart-statement.org). As we describe in detail in Chap. 6, these statements have become subject to increasing controversy, and a lively debate has since ensued on the merits and limits of transparency, especially for different types of qualitative research. As noted by Shih (2015), Driscoll (2015), and Lynch (2016), tensions between transparency obligations and protection of respondents are particularly acute when it comes to fieldwork research in authoritarian circumstances. While these and other contributions have thrown open the debate by critiquing DA-RT, the tension between transparency and protection remains unresolved, and few alternative models have emerged. More recently, European policy-makers have developed even more sweeping proposals to improve 'the accessibility of data and knowledge at all stages of the research cycle' (Directorate-General for Research and Innovation 2016, 52), making it all the more urgent to develop a considered response to such calls for transparency from the perspective of authoritarian field research.

There are no easy fixes either for the tension between transparency and responsibility towards respondents, or to the issues of risk raised by Regeni's death. Without simplifying, this book aims to contribute to improving the practice of authoritarian field research, by laying bare some of the dilemmas and trade-offs we encountered, examining our own decisions with hindsight, and discussing strategies we developed, to make it easier for others. We also want to open the space for reflecting on themes that we believe are too little discussed, let alone written about, by political scientists: our fears, insecurities and mistakes during fieldwork, the mental impact it has on us, and the possibility of coming home with little in the way of publishable findings.

The book is structured in the following way: in this chapter, we explain who we are, define our subject matter, and try to dispel some prejudices and dichotomous ways of thinking. We describe how we wrote the book, and for whom we believe it will be useful. In Chap. 2, we discuss how we enter the field: navigating institutional ethics requirements, getting permission to enter, and preparing for the particularities and risks involved in authoritarianism research. In Chap. 3, we explain the concept of 'red lines': topics that are sensitive or even taboo to discuss in authoritarian contexts, how we learn what they are, and how we navigate them. In Chap. 4, we discuss how we build and maintain relations in the field: how we relate to local collaborators, how we approach respondents and conduct interviews, and the responsibilities we have towards our contacts in the field. Chapter 5 discusses the mental impact of authoritarian field research, which is always stressful, often stimulating, and sometimes involves dealing with surveillance, fear, betrayal, or the suffering of others. We also reflect on adverse consequences of pressure to get results. In Chap. 6 we describe the constraints of the authoritarian field when 'writing up', and our practices concerning anonymization and off-the-record information. We make some concrete proposals on how to deal with the tension between protecting respondents and scientific transparency. In the final pages of the book, we give a carefully qualified list of 'do's and don'ts', distilled from our reflections in each chapter.

Who We Are

This book is a product of the ERC-funded research project *Authoritarianism in a Global Age*, based at the University of Amsterdam, which comprises four postdoctoral researchers, two PhD candidates, a junior researcher, and the principal investigator. For this project, we have done field research on aspects of authoritarianism in China, Iran, Kazakhstan, Malaysia, and Morocco, and on subnational authoritarianism in India and Mexico, from 2015 to 2017. Our inclusion of India and Mexico in this volume requires some explanation: after the transition to democracy of many countries of Latin America in the 1980s and 1990s, political scientists came to the realization that in many of these contexts, the transition remained geographically uneven. Regions and states within a national federation succeeded in remaining authoritarian, even while national-level politics became pluralist and more respectful of civil and political rights. This insight spawned the concepts of 'subnational authoritarianism' or 'subnational undemocratic regions' (O'Donnell 1993; Gibson 2005; Durazo Herrmann 2010; Gervasoni 2010), which have since also been applied to regions in Russia and Kyrgyzstan (McMann 2006), the Philippines (Sidel 2014), and India (Tudor and Ziegfeld 2016). When we refer, in this book, to India and Mexico as authoritarian contexts, we specifically have Gujarat, India, and Veracruz, Mexico, where our fieldwork took place, in mind. But these are not the only subnational authoritarian regions in these two countries, and indeed there are many such regions worldwide. While there are some important empirical and theoretical differences between national authoritarian states and subnational regions, we have found that as *fieldwork contexts*, they are not so different, and we believe that many of our experiences and recommendations are applicable to such regions more generally. In other words, such regions within formal democracies should be treated as 'authoritarian fields'. Indeed, as will become clear, the Veracruz context was probably the most brutally repressive one we investigated in this project. In our broader project, we also investigated the effect authoritarian rule continues to have on its citizens beyond borders (Glasius 2018; Dalmasso 2018; Del Sordi 2018; Michaelsen 2016), and we occasionally refer to this field of research in Europe too. We also draw on our collective fieldwork experience from previous projects, in the countries mentioned above as well as in the authoritarian or transition contexts of Cameroon, Egypt, Indonesia, Pakistan, Tunisia, and the short-lived 'Tamil Eelam' controlled by the Tamil Tigers. Hence, we bring together a tremendous amount of fresh, cross-regional experience in the authoritarian field, as well as rich knowledge of the relevant political science and area studies literature. We have devoted frequent group sessions both to preparing for our fieldwork, and to reflecting on our experiences afterwards. We were helped tremendously with this by the three ethical advisors we sought out to think through our dilemmas: Marcel van der Heijden, program manager at HIVOS and an expert on Central Asia and the Middle East; Dirk Kruijt, professor emeritus at the University of Utrecht and an expert on Latin America and the Caribbean; and Malcolm Smart, a human rights professional who has managed various regional and other programs for Amnesty International, Article 19, and Human Rights Watch. We take this opportunity to thank them for their advice and support. These discussions between ourselves and with our advisors, and the realization that in previous projects we had not had the benefit either of written guidance, or of an exchange of experiences and practices, gave rise to this book.

Our reflections and recommendations in this book are based on our individual experiences. Where many of us have very similar experiences, not only during the fieldwork for this project but also in previous fieldwork episodes, we have taken the liberty of abstracting from these incidents or practices and formulated more general findings. Wherever possible, we have engaged with the existing literature so as to be on firmer ground in our quest for generalization. In many other instances in this book, where our experiences are more varied, contradictory, or even unique, we just describe what our practice is or what has happened to us as an individual experience. Importantly, we want to emphasize that one should not read the experiences of, for instance, our China or Iran researcher, as 'this is what it is like to do field research in China', or 'this has been the experience of political scientists going into Iran'. It is not just the country context but also the political timing of our research; our research agenda; the kinds of respondents we seek out; characteristics such as our gender, age, and nationality; and even our personality that feed into the experiences we have. Nonetheless, even where we are reluctant to generalize from our experience, we believe the collection of incidents and routines we put forward here will be helpful to others in orienting themselves on future fieldwork, or reflecting on past fieldwork, and contributes to building up a sedimentation of experiences in the authoritarian field.

What Is the Authoritarian Field?

The expression 'authoritarian field', which we used for the title of this book, has two different meanings. First of all, it is a field of academic research. As such, it denotes the study of authoritarian rule as an object of research, and those academics, primarily political scientists, who are its students. There are different ways of studying authoritarianism: historically, empirically with quantitative, qualitative, or mixed methods, or (more rarely) purely theoretically. Second, the 'authoritarian field' is a place where academics and others spend time to gather research data. As such, it refers to territories under the jurisdiction of governments that are authoritarian in the senses outlined below: they fail to conduct fully free and fair elections, they curtail freedom of expression and freedom of association, and most importantly for our experience, there is some arbitrariness to their governance, resulting in various forms of insecurity for those who reside in or enter such territories. As we already mentioned, authoritarian jurisdiction is not always coterminous with the borders of a state, and in fact authoritarian power need not be strictly territorial (Glasius 2018; Cooley and Heathershaw 2017), but mostly what we discuss in this book does concern conditions within the borders of an authoritarian polity.

We as authors are 'in the authoritarian field' in both senses: we gather data in places that are under authoritarian rule, and our object of study is also authoritarian rule. For the purposes of this book, we use the expression 'authoritarian field' in the second sense: as a geographical space structured by particular sociopolitical features. When we discuss the authoritarian field as an object of study, we use 'authoritarianism' or 'authoritarian rule'. Along with the rest of the political science profession, we tend sometimes to think of our field as divided into quantitative and qualitative, and to equate the latter orientation with going into the 'authoritarian field' in the second sense. This is an unhelpful oversimplification. It overlooks the contribution of historical studies, which may be desk-based, but may also involve fieldwork to get to relevant archives (see, for instance, Thøgersen 2006; Tsourapas 2015, 2016). Equally, quantitative research can be based on surveys or statistics that can only be gathered in the field. Three of us have experience with conducting surveys in the authoritarian field, and we will reflect on those experiences here. Nonetheless, most of our fieldwork revolves around conducting interviews, which we believe also reflects the most prevalent source of data among our fieldworker colleagues. We therefore focus particularly on interviewing (in Chap. 4) and handling transcripts (in Chap. 6).

How We Experience Authoritarianism

Definitional matters get surprisingly little attention in authoritarianism research, but that is a topic for another publication (Glasius Forthcoming). A minimum definition that political scientists subscribe to is that authoritarianism is characterized by the absence of free and fair competition in elections. The contexts we investigate do indeed have in common the absence of fully free and fair elections. However, for understanding the specific challenges of authoritarian fieldwork, this is not a particularly helpful point of reference. A broader, less universally agreed definition of authoritarianism insists that apart from the lack of free and fair elections, authoritarian regimes are also characterized by violations of the right to freedom of expression and access to information, and freedom of association. This begins to give us some better clues as to the specificity of the authoritarian field, but it too provides limited insight into what the authoritarian field is like as a research context.

In other publications, we have provided analyses of many aspects of the various authoritarian regimes we study. Here, we want to take the opportunity to share something we cannot fully communicate in our substantive work: how we *experience* authoritarianism in our fieldwork. While a focus on elections simply is not relevant for understanding everyday life, a focus on civil rights violations might cause us to envisage authoritarian-ruled states as giant prison camps. We may get fixated on a notion of agents of the state who are constantly and single-mindedly involved in arresting dissidents, harassing journalists, closing down websites or breaking up demonstrations. Indeed, some of us have found that by using authoritarianism as an analytical lens, we unintentionally constructed a monster in our minds called authoritarian regime. The monster, we imagined, is out to do nasty things to its citizens, and perhaps to us. All of the governments we study do curtail freedom of expression and association, but they also pursue educational policies, regulate export licenses, and worry about the economy; and their officials also attend summits, give rousing speeches, and attend to personnel matters. While there are examples of authoritarian regimes in which all citizens live in fear of their governments all the time (North Korea is the paradigmatic example), the twenty-first century authoritarian governance we study is more subtle, and uses repressive measures more sparingly. As first-time visitors, some of us needed to experience that most people are not being arrested most of the time, before being able to discern the more subtle ways in which the environment *is* authoritarian. This has not been our universal experience, however. Our Kazakhstan researcher, by contrast, having lived in Kazakhstan before she became an academic, was inclined to separate the analytical lens of 'authoritarianism' from everyday experiences in the country, and only gradually became more aware of the potential risks attached to her research. Our China researcher, having grown up in the People's Republic, did not need to discover the multidimensional realities of China, having experienced them from birth.

Our initial prejudices may also have led us into truncated moral judgments, assuming that (all) agents of the state are the bad guys, corrupt and repressive, and (all) activists are the good guys. We needed to discover that agents of the state can be conscientious, well-informed, and willing to discuss the problems of their political system with us, as well as sometimes inviting us to look critically at the policies of democratic countries. Activists, we found, are often brave and impressive but can also at times be vain, petty, and invested in criticizing their peers as much as the government. Another bias some of us have had to shed relates to the aspirations of citizens of authoritarian countries. Some citizens of authoritarian states do think that life is 'better' in democratic countries, and they would like to live there if they could, but many do not. Our Kazakhstan researcher found that for Kazakhstani students who went to study in democratic countries, being in an environment where civil liberties are respected was not automatically relevant and important to most of them. Our Iran researcher found that even for Iranian citizens who *do* deeply value human rights and personal freedoms, this does not necessarily mean they would like to go and live in the west if they could. They want to stay and change their own country, and if they have to leave, it is with a heavy heart.

The feature of authoritarianism that most prominently affects our fieldwork is not its repressive aspect as such, but its arbitrariness, and the uncertainty that results in for us and the people in our fieldwork environment. In democratic contexts, without knowing in detail all the laws of the land, we have a reasonable understanding of what is legal and what is criminal behavior. In authoritarian circumstances, it is never quite so clear what you can and cannot do. There are laws, many laws, but they are not consistently applied, they contradict each other, and executive behavior without legal sanction is also a possibility. This results in a sense of uncertainty: you never know whether you are crossing a red line or not (for a longer discussion of the concept of 'red lines', see Chap. 3). In fact, the insecurity cuts both ways. People within the regime also suffer from uncertainty, about the level of popular legitimacy and robustness of their regime, even in ostensibly very stable circumstances (an insight reflected in the title of Andreas Schedler's book *The Politics of Uncertainty*, 2013). Our presence as researchers is probably a low priority within the constellation of self-perceived existential threats to the regime, but we cannot take this for granted. Most of the time, we probably will not be crossing a red line, but the lines are not fixed; they move, for us and for our respondents. In all probability, nothing will happen. But the latent threat that something can happen, to you or your respondents, is what is specific about authoritarian regimes, and hence also authoritarian fieldwork. Finally, the authoritarian field may have a cultural element: authoritarianism is not only about what the state or the party does but also about how people have internalized self-limitation, even while the concrete limits of free speech are set by the leadership, and subject to change. The arbitrary behavior of the state brings about feelings of mistrust, powerlessness, and uncertainty in people which can affect their social relations, with each other and with us.

Beyond 'Westerners' and 'Locals'

In a book like this, reflecting on our fieldwork experiences, we tend to fall into thinking in terms of a stereotypical dichotomy: us, westerners, who go to visit them, the locals, in their field. It is true that the authors of this book all are, or have been, employed at western universities, and we do go on fieldwork in authoritarian contexts, sometimes for months, but we do not live there. But our identities and relations to the field are a bit more varied than the dichotomy would suggest. As already mentioned, our China researcher grew up in the 'field' she researches. She needed time to acclimatize to the culture and politics of Europe, and now approaches the field with more of a sense of distance, but she is not 'a westerner' any more than she is 'a local'. Our Iran researcher, ostensibly a 'westerner' with his German passport, in fact also grew up in an 'authoritarian field': the German Democratic Republic. Our Kazakhstan researcher feels that growing up in Southern Italy, while certainly not authoritarian, does not fit stereotypical ideas of western liberal democracy either. The crucial importance of informal networks in her region of origin resembles that in the Kazakh political field. We mention these biographical details because we see them reflected in the often complex identities and relations to the field of many of our colleagues: some are nationals of the fields they study, many have dual nationality (this seems to be especially prevalent among Iran scholars), some have spouses with origins in 'the field', some have grown up in it, and so on.

Conversely, as anthropologists have long noted, the 'locals' are not invariably rooted to the soil of the authoritarian field. We are acutely aware of this because the mobility of nationals of authoritarian countries is part of our substantive research agenda. Many of the Iranian journalists and bloggers who came to form our Iran researcher's local network a decade ago have fled the country after the 2009 crackdown on election protests, and now live all over the world. Our Kazakhstan researcher has interviewed Kazakhstani students during a period of study abroad, or after their return, and our China researcher does survey research on Chinese students' experience abroad. Our Morocco researcher has done research among Moroccans in the Netherlands, Belgium, and France. Hence, we do not find colonial images of us, intrepid travelers, who go to visit the natives and report back on how they behave, to correspond to our actual experiences. Nor do we suffer much from postcolonial guilt. In some cases, we experience that we are in a relation of economic privilege in relation to our respondents, but mostly, we do not. Most of the authoritarian countries we investigate are not particularly poor countries, and our respondents are not usually the marginalized in society, but members of the middle class, sometimes even the elite. We recognize that this may be different for researchers in other authoritarian contexts, or with different research agendas. Researching the authoritarian regimes of extremely poor countries, such as Eritrea or Tajikistan, or vulnerable groups, such as undocumented migrants, religious minorities, or indigenous people, may throw up ethical questions that we have not had to face. Nonetheless, we are privileged in a political sense: our affiliations to western universities, and for most of us our passports, often give us greater protection from the authoritarian state than its residents have. Moreover, if we ever feel that the authoritarian field gets to be too oppressive or dangerous to us, we can get on a plane, usually from one day to the next, and get beyond the reach of the state we study. None of us have had to exercise that option, but it is there. For most of the people we come into contact with, it is not.

How We Wrote This Book

Writing a book with eight people is not like writing alone or with a small number of co-authors, but it can be done. In fact we recommend the experience for research groups that have worked closely together, as a way of capturing the accumulated knowledge. Since we all use interviews as our primary material in our own research, we naturally turned to interviews as the most appropriate way to structure the writing process: we interviewed ourselves. We first brainstormed about what topics should be covered in the book and came to a provisional table of contents. Then, the project leader and the project assistant came up with a list of interview questions, which was amended by the six other researchers, who have done all the fieldwork in this project. The project assistant proceeded to have in-depth interviews with the six researchers, often over two sessions, yielding about eighteen hours of interview material. The six field researchers edited the project assistant's interview transcripts and cut and pasted them into the table of contents. The project assistant also placed relevant passages from existing literature into this format. The project leader then produced first drafts of each chapter, which were in turn discussed with, and edited and commented on by, the six field researchers. We also commissioned comments from a number of our colleagues at the University of Amsterdam, all experienced fieldworkers, on different draft chapters. We would like to thank Julia Bader, Farid Boussaid, Marieke de Goede, Julian Gruin, Imke Harbers, Beste Isleyen, Vivienne Matthies-Boon, Polly Pallister-Wilkins, Abbey Steele, and Nel Vandekerckhove for their comments. After a second round of edits, the full text was submitted for review. We gratefully acknowledge our anonymous reviewer for the helpful comments, both on the proposal and on the draft manuscript of the book.

Who This Book Is For

This book should be essential reading to those readers who, like the authors, are in the authoritarian field in both senses. For academics who study authoritarianism on the basis of desk-based research, this book will help them to better understand the ways of working of their colleagues who do fieldwork, and perhaps consider it for themselves, or in collaboration, in mixed-methods projects. Fieldwork research has in the past sometimes been treated as an art form rather than a method, something that cannot be taught. While we do think it involves a certain amount of learning by doing, we do not want it to be approached as an occult pursuit. We expect this book to be especially useful for junior scholars, such as PhD researchers or researchers exploring the topic of authoritarianism for the first time, but we aspire to speak to senior scholars as well. Even if the recent reflective turn in qualitative methods comes too late for you to be 'trained' in them, it is never too late to explicitly reflect on the merits and drawbacks of one's approach to field research, and our work can serve as a source of comparison in this respect.

The first four chapters of this book will also be valuable to academics who (aim to) spend time in the authoritarian field but whose research does not revolve around authoritarianism. Social scientists who study agricultural or trade policy, forest management, gender, or religion in authoritarian contexts are likely at some point to find themselves confronted with the sensitivities of the authoritarian state. Even beyond the social sciences, scholars of archeology, climate change, or epidemiology who are in the authoritarian field will need to have some engagement with local policymakers, and will profit from having a social awareness of the context in which they find themselves. Researchers may find themselves caught in politics, even though they never intended to investigate the political aspects of a given topic. We can think, for instance, of a linguist studying the Tamazight languages of North Africa, who suddenly finds that her extensive contact with the people who speak it is a source of suspicion to the authorities, or a biologist who is interested in the fish population in the Yangtze river and discovers that the disappearance of certain species due to pollution is a politically sensitive topic.

Chapters 5 and 6, which deal with mental impact and with anonymization of sources respectively, will be of interest to other categories of scholars. Academics who work with vulnerable groups in society, such as drug users, sex workers, or undocumented migrants, or with groups that engage in illegal or controversial behaviors, such as criminal gangs or racist movements, may be confronted with the negative mental impact of living through traumatic incidents or hearing hard stories. The same may be true for scholars who investigate the repressive or secretive aspects of democratic states, such as the practices of secret services, anti-terrorist policies, or counterinsurgency training. Scholarship on all these topics also faces the challenge of how to deal with anonymity in the face of an increasing call for transparency, just as we do, and they may consider to what extent our practices and recommendations are applicable for their fields.

Finally, beyond the academy, we expect some chapters of this book to make useful reading for policy-makers, civil society practitioners, business people, or journalists who find themselves in the authoritarian field, or dealing with authoritarian state authorities. Some may have a more difficult experience: as we describe in more detail in Chaps. 2 and 4, there are important differences between our work and that of journalists and human rights investigators in particular, which may cause them to have a harder time. On the other hand, valued technical experts or cultural journalists may experience much less in the way of political impediments or sensitivities than we have done. Nonetheless, for anyone who expects to have significant interactions with locals in the authoritarian field, there is relevant guidance in this book regarding the need to spend time getting used to the sociopolitical as much as the physical climate (Chap. 2), to develop a sensitivity to the 'red lines' (Chap. 3), and to build trust with interlocutors (Chap. 4). Chapter 5 may be of interest to human rights and humanitarian workers, to compare our experiences and recommendations to the practices that have been developed in their own fields. Chapter 6 may be of interest to journalists, who face similar trade-offs between protecting sources and being transparent.

References

Cooley, A., & Heathershaw, J. (2017). *Dictators Without Borders Power and Money in Central Asia*. New Haven: Yale University Press.

Dalmasso, E. (2018). Participation Without Representation. Moroccans Abroad at a Time of Unstable Authoritarian Rule. Special Issue on The Authoritarian Rule of Populations Abroad. *Globalizations*.

Del Sordi, A. (2018). Sponsoring Student Mobility for Development *and* Authoritarian Stability: Kazakhstan's Bolashak Program. Special Issue on The Authoritarian Rule of Populations Abroad. *Globalizations*.

Directorate-General Research & Innovation. (2016). Open Innovation, Open Science, Open to the World. *European Commission*. Retrieved from https://publications.europa.eu/en/publication-detail/-/publication/3213b335-1cbc-11e6-ba9a-01aa75ed71a1.

Driscoll, J. (2015). Can Anonymity Promises Possibly Be Credible In Police States? In M. Golder & S. N. Golder (Eds.), *Comparative Politics Newsletter. Comparative Politics of the American Political Science Association*, *25*, 4–7.

Durazo Herrmann, J. (2010). Neo-Patrimonialism and Subnational Authoritarianism in Mexico. The Case of Oaxaca. *Journal of Politics in Latin America, 2*, 85–112. Retrieved from http://journals.sub.uni-hamburg.de/giga/jpla/article/view/276/276.

Gervasoni, C. (2010). Measuring Variance in Subnational Regimes: Results from an Expert-Based Operationalization of Democracy in the Argentine Provinces. *Journal of Politics in Latin America, 2*, 13–52.

Gibson, E. (2005). Boundary Control: Subnational Authoritarianism in Democratic Countries. *World Politics, 58*, 101–132.

Glasius, M. (2018). Extraterritorial Authoritarian Practices: a Framework. Special Issue on The Authoritarian Rule of Populations Abroad. *Globalizations.*

Glasius, M. (Forthcoming). What Authoritarianism Is … and Is Not: A Practice Perspective.

Goode, J. P., & Ahram, A. I. (2016). Special Issue Editors' Introduction: Observing Autocracies from the Ground Floor. *Social Science Quarterly, 97*, 823–833. https://doi.org/10.1111/ssqu.12339.

Heimer, M., & Thøgersen, S. (Eds.). (2006). *Doing Fieldwork in China.* Copenhagen: NIAS Press.

Hilhorst, D., Hodgson, L., Jansen, B., & Mena, R. (2016). *Security Guidelines for Field Research in Complex, Remote and Hazardous Places.* The Hague: ISS-EUR. Retrieved from https://www.iss.nl/news_events/iss_news/detail_news/news/5486-security-guidelines-for-researchers/.

Koch, N. (2013). Introduction – Field Methods in "Closed Contexts": Undertaking Research in Authoritarian States and Places. *Area, 45*, 390–339. https://doi.org/10.1111/area.12044.

Lynch, M. (2016). Area Studies and the Cost of Prematurely Implementing DA-RT. In M. Golder & S. N. Golder (Eds.), *Comparative Politics Newsletter. Comparative Politics of the American Political Science Association, 26*, 36–40.

Mazurana, D., Jacobsen, K., & Gale, L. A. (Eds.). (2013). *Research Methods in Conflict Settings.* New York: Cambridge University Press.

McMann, K. M. (2006). *Economic Autonomy and Democracy: Hybrid Regimes in Russia and Kyrgyzstan.* Cambridge: Cambridge University Press.

Michaelsen, M. (2016). Exit and Voice in the Digital Age: Iran's Exiled Activists and the Authoritarian State. Special Issue on The Authoritarian Rule of Populations Abroad. *Globalizations.* https://doi.org/10.1080/14747731.2016.1263078. [details].

O'Donnell, G. (1993). On the State, Democratization, and Some Conceptual Problems: A Latin American View with Glances at Some Postcommunist Countries. *World Development, 21*, 1355–1369.

Schedler, A. (2013). *The Politics of Uncertainty: Sustaining and Subverting Electoral Authoritarianism.* New York: Oxford University Press.

Shih, V. (2015). Research in Authoritarian Regimes: Transparency Tradeoffs and Solutions. In T. Buthe & A. M. Jacobs (Eds.), *Qualitative and Multi-Method Research. American Political Science Association, 13*, 20–22.

Sidel, J. T. (2014). The Philippines in 2013: Disappointment, Disgrace, Disaster. *Asian Survey, 54*, 64–70.

Sriram, C. L., King, J. C., & Mertus, J. A. (Eds.). (2009). *Surviving Field Research: Working in Violent and Difficult Situations.* Oxford: Routledge.

Thomson, S., Ansoms, A., & Murison, J. (Eds.). (2013). *Emotional and Ethical Challenges for Field Research in Africa: The Story Behind the Findings.* London: Palgrave Macmillan.

Thøgersen, S. (2006). Approaching the Field Through Written Sources. In M. Heimer & S. Thøgersen (Eds.), *Doing Fieldwork in China* (pp. 189–205). Copenhagen: NIAS Press.

Tsourapas, G. (2015). Why Do States Develop Multi-Tier Emigrant Policies? Evidence from Egypt. *Journal of Ethnic & Migration Studies, 41*, 2192–2214.

Tsourapas, G. (2016). Nasser's Educators and Agitators Across al-Watan al-'Arabi: Tracing the Foreign Policy Importance of Egyptian Regional Migration, 1952–1967. *British Journal of Middle Eastern Studies, 43*, 324–341.

Tudor, M., & Ziegfeld, A. (2016). Sub-national Democratization in India: The Role of Competition and Central Intervention. In L. Whitehead & J. Behrend (Eds.), *Illiberal Practices: Territorial Variance Within Large Federal Democracies.* Baltimore: Johns Hopkins Press.

CHAPTER 2

Entering the Field

Abstract In this chapter, we deal with authoritarian field research in relation to ethics procedures (or lack thereof!), visas, and permits, and what we do in advance to prepare for an optimal, and optimally safe, fieldwork period. We acknowledge that fieldwork in authoritarian contexts is mostly not very dangerous for researchers, but it can be. We discuss the particular nature of authoritarian fieldwork risks, the concrete risks we ourselves and others have faced, and what we can do to assess and mitigate those risks. We conclude that while we should be aware of risk and try to minimize it, we need to accept that risk cannot be eliminated if we want to engage in authoritarian fieldwork.

Keywords Authoritarianism • Field research • Risk • Fieldwork ethics • Safety • Access

In this chapter, we discuss our preparations for entering the field and our handling of the risks associated with authoritarian fieldwork. In terms of preparations, we deal with experiences with the ethics procedures (or lack thereof!) of universities and funders, the vagaries of visa requirements, and what we do in advance to prepare for an optimal, and optimally safe, fieldwork period. We discuss the particular nature of authoritarian fieldwork risks, the concrete risks we ourselves and others have faced, and what we

M. Glasius et al., *Research, Ethics and Risk in the Authoritarian Field*,
https://doi.org/10.1007/978-3-319-68966-1_2

can do to assess and mitigate those risks. We will conclude that while we should be aware of risk and try to minimize it, we need to accept that it cannot be eliminated if we want to engage in authoritarian fieldwork.

Ethics Procedures

Authoritarian field research poses a number of ethical challenges. The most prominent of these is undoubtedly the potential risk to our respondents, but risk to ourselves, issues of informed consent, and potential misuse of findings by authoritarian regimes are also among them. We deal with such issues, and with what we hold to constitute ethical behavior, throughout this book. But we also operate in institutional environments, which sometimes come with their own ethical review procedures. We have found great variance in the appropriateness and comprehensiveness of such procedures. We recognize a general reflex among academics to consider ethical review as just another bureaucratic nuisance. However, it is our shared experience that, when well-designed, ethical reviews can be extremely useful in pushing us to reflect on ethical implications of our research. Our Kazakhstan researcher, for instance, asked colleagues who had done fieldwork research in Central Asia before what they had done to keep interview material confidential, and whether they had trained research assistants on ethical matters, in order to meet the ethics requirements of her co-author's US university, which funded the research. She would never have asked colleagues these questions if the Internal Review Board's questions had not required her to describe the procedures she would use. We also have some experience with less appropriate ethical review procedures, and considerable experience with a complete absence of ethical review procedures.

We have on occasion experienced ethical review as a bureaucratic nuisance ourselves: our current funder, the European Research Council (ERC), for instance insisted, after most of the fieldwork had already taken place, on receiving a copy of the interview protocols of each our field researchers. We dutifully supplied sample protocols for each researcher, but we do not believe these to be particularly meaningful. As every qualitative researcher knows, every interview is slightly different from the last, and we never stick precisely to the script. We also have some doubt as to whether the ethics auditors who asked for the interview guides actually went on to peruse them. This example, we would put in the category of harmless bureaucratic nuisance: we do not think the request was particularly useful, but it did not cost us a huge amount of time, and it did not in any way interfere with our own views of what is ethical.

Ethical review procedures can become really problematic, however, when their existence actually causes us to behave less ethically than we otherwise would. This can come about in response to 'one-size-fits-all' procedures, without an understanding of the particularities of qualitative social science research in general, or of the specific challenges of authoritarian field research. Much depends on who conducts the review. Thus, our funder, the ERC, uses a form that asks whether 'the proposal meets the national legal and ethical requirements of the country where the research will be performed' and whether 'approval of the proposed study by a relevant authority at national level' will be sought. Fortunately, our ethical auditors ticked both boxes as 'yes', while indicating in writing their acceptance of our explanations why we could not guarantee to always be in compliance with national law, or get formal approval from state authorities (see also below). They also accepted our argument that under the circumstances, oral consent was more appropriate than signatures on consent forms (see also Wall and Overton 2006, 64). Had the ethics review been conducted by someone with less understanding of the particularities of authoritarianism research, we might have had difficulties getting clearance. We do not know of any instances where an ethical review procedure actually prohibited a scholar from undertaking authoritarian field research (but see Matelski 2014, who mentions a case relating to Myanmar). A more frequently encountered problem is that, by making impossible requests, review boards may actually 'encourage obfuscation' rather than transparency (Wall and Overton 2006, 62). We know of a colleague working in African contexts for instance, who had been taught by his well-respected PhD supervisor to produce counterfeit informed consent forms, because their university required them, even in contexts where they would be quite inappropriate and perhaps even unethical.

While we have no personal experience of ethical reviews making impossible demands, we have considerable experience of operating in universities that have no ethical review procedures whatsoever. Three of the four postdoctoral researchers in our project encountered neither ethics procedures nor any ethics training during their PhD trajectory. Our Morocco researcher went on to work for two other European universities without encountering any institutional engagement with research ethics. The researchers in question do not believe they have made fatal ethical mistakes in their research, but the lack of institutional awareness of ethical concerns did sometimes make them feel unprepared for problems and dilemmas they encountered in the field. Moreover, it meant that there was no obvious person or body to consult on these matters; they were left to figure them out on their own, without much experience.

In general then, we would argue for engaged ethics procedures, preferably with an element of human interaction, that force us to reflect on ethical challenges we might encounter without turning into a bureaucratic box-ticking exercise. We would urge academics to push for such procedures, not only when they face procedures that are too rigid but also where they encounter an absence of either training or clearance reviews.

Gaining Entry: Permits and Visas

As part of the ethics procedures described above, some universities and grant-making institutions insist that researchers should seek prior permission to do research from some authority in the country where their fieldwork is to take place. There may, in general, be circumstances in which requiring such permission is quite justified, for instance, when doing research related to a country's natural resources or conducting medical trials. When it comes to the social sciences, we believe that there is no general justifiable need for such permission, but there may be circumstances in which it is reasonable for the state to limit entry. Loyle (2016, 927), for instance, describes how Rwanda instituted a permit system 'in part as a response to rampant and unchecked social and scientific research that was conducted in the country post-1994 with limited regard for the health and psychological well-being of research participants'. Today however, Loyle points out, the 'process serves as a high-cost barrier to research in Rwanda', and severely constrains research on subjects of sensitivity to the government.

Below we describe some of our own practices when gaining entry, and the restrictions and ambiguities in state policies on permission for research we encountered. With one exception, none of us have ever sought government permission for our research on authoritarianism, or applied for a research visa. Such an official request, if there is even a dedicated procedure to process it, would only serve to attract the authorities' attention to our research, arouse suspicion, and most likely result in a denial. For Morocco, for instance, there is a procedure, and one is formally required to ask for permission to do research in the country. But getting permission can take months and sometimes it is just not given. To our knowledge, most Maghreb researchers do not apply for it. India officially requires a research visa, but despite being formally democratic, it is very restrictive in giving out visas for any politically sensitive research, such as in our case repression in the context of subnational authoritarianism, but also, for instance, on the Maoist insurgency or other armed groups, or any research on Kashmir.

Our first visit to the field was often different from subsequent experiences in terms of our purpose for going. Our Iran researcher came primarily to study the language, our Kazakhstan researcher was working for an international organization, and our India researcher felt that, as a master student, the line between just 'hanging out' as someone who is interested in the country and being there as an academic researcher was still quite fluid. Once we were set on our career course, this kind of convenient ambiguity has tended to dissipate. Even our China researcher, a Chinese national who grew up in the country, now clearly goes as a researcher, not just someone visiting home.

So, how do we enter the country nowadays? Sometimes, we go on tourist visa. Tourist-friendly countries like Malaysia, Morocco, or Mexico make it very easy to enter the country—indeed Europeans can stay in Morocco for three months without even applying for a visa. There is something uneasy about doing research on a tourist visa or without a permit, especially where a research visa or permit does in fact exist. But a tourist visa does not imply that we are treating the purpose of our presence as a secret. We all carry letters from our home universities, signed by a head of department or university official, explaining our research, but we have rarely had occasion to produce them. Our Morocco researcher writes 'study, work and tourism' or 'work and tourism' on her immigration form. Our India and Mexico researcher has conducted interviews with local policemen and magistrates while on a tourist visa. The experience is that state officials are not in the habit of questioning whether one has a research visa or permit: how you came into the country is not really their concern. Nonetheless, the lack of an official stamp of approval can make us vulnerable, or at least make us feel vulnerable. Our Morocco researcher applied for official approval for her research on Salafists after experiencing intrusive surveillance, an experience detailed in Chap. 5. She applied not because she expected to get permission (and indeed she never received a response to the request) but simply in order to signal that she was not doing clandestine research.

For other countries, such as China, Iran, or Kazakhstan, getting any type of visa requires more bureaucratic effort, and moreover, there is a realistic risk of being denied entry. To some of us, the restrictive visa policies seem like part and parcel of the system of authoritarian control: the government wants to strictly monitor who enters, and who does what in the country. In post-Soviet countries in particular, it is not just the entry visa. One needs to regularly register one's exact whereabouts, with a hotel or with the migration police. Having said that, as western researchers we may too easily read authoritarianism into such requirements, and forget the often draconian procedures of our own authorities vis-à-vis non-residents. Our China researcher, when she first came to the United Kingdom from China, also had to register with the local authorities at the police station.

An important commonality in our experiences with gaining entry is ambiguity: the rules are unclear, they keep changing, or they are applied unevenly. Our Iran researcher is pretty certain that the lack of response to his request for a study visa in 2015 was not politically motivated, but just a matter of sloppiness, the application had been delayed or forgotten somewhere, and he was quickly issued a tourist visa instead. At the same time, Iran researchers do regularly have their visa denied on what are likely to be political grounds. Even some researchers with long-term relationships and networks have still been denied. Our China researcher can freely leave and enter the country, but she has seen that the treatment of foreign scholars by the Chinese government appears quite arbitrary: a colleague whose visa application was rejected reapplied two weeks later and was accepted. A US-based scholar working on Tibet was rejected, which seems unsurprising in itself, but then another researcher working on the same topic was accepted at almost the same time. In Kazakhstan, entry has actually become easier in recent years, with visa-free regimes offered for short stays. But the bottom line, in Kazakhstan as in other authoritarian contexts, is that the bureaucratic requirements are never quite stable and transparent, and this in itself creates the kind of legal uncertainty that appears to be one of the hallmarks of authoritarian rule. Most authoritarianism scholars gain access to their fieldwork sites most of the time, but denial of entry is always a possibility, and even expulsion is never unthinkable.

Constrained Choices

Our choices of fieldwork countries, and of research topics, are in part determined by what is possible, and safe. Little is in fact known about what drives fieldwork choices. Clark's (2006) valuable survey of difficulties faced by researchers in the Middle East and North Africa only showed 16% of respondents specifying 'the political situation' and safety as contributing to their country choices, and did not distinguish between repression and other safety risks. A more recent study on the political risks of field research in Central Asia found that '(s)everal respondents reported that they no longer work in Uzbekistan' and a 'few respondents singled out Turkmenistan and Azerbaijan as sites where they have experienced significant censorship/restrictions, chosen not to go, or experienced difficulty going'(CESS 2016, 7). Goode (2010) initially discerned a relation between Russia becoming more autocratic and a decline in fieldwork, but qualified his conclusions in a later study of the broader region (Goode 2016). Nonetheless, we would logically expect the most repressive regimes within the authoritarian universe to be less likely settings for field research: either because it would be too dangerous, or simply because it is impossible to gain access. Similarly, assessments of feasibility and risk are likely to constrain the choice of research topics and research questions. We do not expand on this point, since it has been dealt with extensively by the contributions to *Observing Autocracies from the Ground Floor* (Goode and Ahram 2016). At the level of our own considerations and observations of colleagues, the notion of constrained country choices, and associated knowledge gaps, seems to have validity. Our Kazakhstan researcher for instance made a clear choice, within Central Asia, not to do research in Uzbekistan for safety reasons. We know no one who has done fieldwork in Saudi Arabia, Turkmenistan, or North Korea. We know colleagues who have started doing research in Myanmar only after it democratized from 2011. And more dramatically, we know many colleagues who have abruptly stopped doing research in Egypt when it became much more repressive in recent years.

Not So Dangerous

Field research in authoritarian settings is by no means the most dangerous kind of social science research one can imagine. Research on organized crime, or in the middle of civil war, is likely to be more dangerous. The risks that a foreign academic runs in an authoritarian country are also incomparable to the risks run by local activists, because of both components, 'foreign' and 'academic'. We write academic books and journals, the tone is balanced, the jargon complex. We do not usually express outrage in our academic work. Moreover, more often than not, we write in

English and not in a local language that is easily accessible to the population. Both foreign journalists and local academics are typically more at risk than we are. A different matter is the risk we may pose to our respondents, an issue we consider in more depth in Chaps. 4 and 6.

Gentile distinguishes between two types of security risk in authoritarian contexts: 'crime-related risks, [in which] the state is, or at least should be, your "friend"' and 'risks in which the state (the secret services, internal security forces and the like) is your "enemy"' (Gentile 2013, 427). We would add two further categories: risks resulting from crisis situations and risks that are related to the authoritarian contexts in more indirect or ambiguous ways. We do not discuss the first type of risk, which does not specifically relate to our position as researchers in the authoritarian field. Along with all other preparations, researchers should of course make themselves aware of the crime profile of the places where they are to do research and take relevant precautions. We devote most attention to the first, 'classic authoritarian' type of risk, but will also address 'crisis risk' and 'indirect risk'.

Depending on which county one investigates, and especially which topic, a researcher may need to prepare for being under electronic or physical surveillance (see also Chap. 5), for being interviewed by security agents (see Gentile 2013), and for being warned off certain activities or topics. All these things have happened to us. It is rare for a researcher to be arrested, detained, or expelled, and slightly less rare but still unusual to be denied entry. These things have not happened to us. Clark's (2006) survey, mentioned above, despite the modest number of responses (55) gives some insight into the frequency of such events, at least in the Middle East and North Africa: '22% of the researchers noted that they at one point had difficulties gaining entry to the countries of research or obtaining research visas due to the perceived political sensitivity of their topics by the host governments. Others reported that they had experienced the threat or actual seizure of their research data (5%), surveillance and monitoring by security (4%), arrest and/or detention (4%), and police harassment (2%)'. The recent Central Asia survey, without giving exact percentages, similarly reports 'ten first-hand accounts of arrest and detention by state officials and a further seventeen of various forms of harassment of the researcher or assistants' among a few hundred respondents (CESS 2016, 8).

Ahram and Goode (2016, 839) discuss the case of 13 China scholars who were denied visas after publishing a book on Xinjiang province, as well as the arrest of Alexander Sodiqov, a PhD student who was arrested on suspicion of treason and held for over a month in Tajikistan (Goode and Ahram 2016, 828). Another incident that has attracted much attention is that of the immediate expulsion of Davenport and Stam (2009) from Rwanda after presenting findings on the genocide that were uncomfortable to the government. There have also been a few recent cases of expulsion of Russia scholars, specifically those who study archives, but according to the US embassy in Moscow, the incidents concern a 'very small minority of the large number of Western academics who travel and study in Russia' (Schreck 2015). While it is difficult to generalize about visa denials, expulsion remains a matter of relative rarity, and arrest even more so, in most authoritarian contexts.

And Yet It Can Be Dangerous

There have been some very worrying recent cases of arrest and detention of social scientists in Iran. Homa Hoodfar, an anthropologist, was held for almost four months and then released in 2016. She coped with prison brutality by dealing with the situation as unintended 'fieldwork' (Kassam 2016). Most recently and dramatically, Xiyue Wang, a PhD student in history at Princeton University, was sentenced to ten years' imprisonment on charges of spying after having already spent a year in prison (Gladstone 2017).

So far, we have not distinguished between foreign visitors such as Davenport and Stam, and dual nationals or nationals investigating their own country, such as Sodiqov or Hoodfar. Since we are dealing with rare occurrences, we cannot systematically compare, but it seems likely that the latter two groups and especially nationals are likely to be more vulnerable to the risks we have outlined, since their treatment is less likely to lead to diplomatic intervention, even though their home university might exert itself on their behalf. Moreover, even apart from the risk of arrest, the impact of expulsion or visa denial on them may be much greater, entailing not just an enforced change of country specialism but being cut off from homeland and loved ones. As for local academics, they fall into a different category altogether, which is not the subject of this book. For them, many research topics are likely to be proscribed, and in most cases, research on their country's authoritarian system as such will not be possible.

The death of Giulio Regeni, a PhD student at the University of Cambridge who was tortured to death whilst doing fieldwork on trade unionism in Egypt in 2016, sent shockwaves through our community of researchers. It was one of the reasons that propelled us to write this book. He was killed for doing exactly what we do. Contrary to some portrayals in the press, Regeni was neither a clueless student, nor did he have a subversive political agenda. He was in close touch with academics who had tremendous local knowledge and made no obvious mistakes. Regeni became the victim of a rapidly deteriorating situation, in which mid-level security agents may have had, or seized, more autonomy than is usual in authoritarian settings. Regeni's death and the responses to it highlight the rarity of such an extreme act of repression against a foreign scholar, and reminds us of our relative safety in comparison to our respondents in the countries we study. Generally, it continues to be true that it is a terrible publicity for a regime to harm a researcher from a western university, and therefore highly unlikely. But Regeni's death is also a reminder that in doing authoritarian field research, we must accept a small risk that things go horribly wrong. The likelihood of such incidents is very low when the regime is stable, but increases in crisis times when the regime feels threatened and needs to reassert its power, such as in the aftermath of the Arab revolts, the Iranian Green Movement protests, or the Andijan massacre in Uzbekistan. Of course if we can predict looming periods of instability in advance, we may (despite the fascination such periods hold for us as political scientists) opt to refrain from doing fieldwork at such times. But one of the hallmarks of authoritarian rule is its apparent unassailability, sometimes followed by sudden collapse, and scholars have had notorious difficulty predicting such collapse. So, we must accept the chance of unexpected crises, and concomitant uncharacteristic behavior from state agents, as one of the known unknowns associated with authoritarian field research.

Possibly the most dangerous work within our group was carried out within an ostensibly democratic context (at least at the national level): in Veracruz, Mexico. The research focused on the subnational authoritarian rule of this region, and in particular on the repression of critical journalists, several of whom had been found murdered in the previous years. The risks he anticipated were only in part connected to the subnational authoritarian context and the researcher's plans. A white young man could be taken for an oil executive (lucrative for kidnapping purposes), or, more connected to politically sensitive interviewing, for a US Drug Enforcement Agency (DEA) official. An important generalizable point here is that there is no obvious correlation (nor, we hasten to add, an inverse correlation) between how authoritarian a state or regional context is and how vulnerable a researcher may be to criminal violence.

Assessing Risk in Advance

One obvious source of information in preparing for fieldwork in authoritarian contexts is human rights reports, or conversations with human rights activists. A problem with this kind of information, however, is that it reports on only one dimension of a multidimensional political system: its human rights record. The purpose of human rights reports is not to give a would-be researcher a balanced and personalized sense of risk. It is important for researchers to know about censorship and about dissidents in prison but also to get past identifying a regime solely with its censors and prisons, especially when their research questions focus on issues other than repression. When a human rights organization uses an expression like 'culture of fear', for instance, we should take it seriously, but not assume a priori that we will indeed find all our potential respondents terrified. Only particular groups will come in for harsh repression, and our likely respondents may not belong to such groups. As Pepinsky has written about Malaysia, in many contexts, '(m)ost not-very-vocal critics will live their lives completely unmolested by the security forces', and will find living under authoritarianism 'tolerable' (Pepinsky 2017).

A similar caveat should be made about the security briefings of our foreign ministries. They are typically written with tourists, perhaps businesspeople in mind, and tend to err on the side of caution in case of any political instability. At the same time, they are not geared towards the very particular risk assessments we need to make. While it is a good idea to contact one's national embassy upon arrival, it is important to be aware that the duties of embassy staff are (a) to maintain good relations with the host country and (b) to be responsible for their nationals when there is any kind of difficulty. Both of these roles may cause them to be conservative in their advice, and not overenthusiastic about political science research undertaken by their nationals. Just like the information from human rights NGOs, the advice from embassies should be seriously considered, but there are good reasons not to make it your primary behavioral guide (see also Loyle 2016, 928).

The best source of information for first-time visitors may be more experienced academics, especially those who have recently been in the field themselves. While some may display gatekeeper behavior, most will be encouraging and helpful. Loyle (2016, 929) also recommends 'works of fiction and journalistic non-fiction', and especially fiction by local authors. If they exist in a language accessible to you, such sources can be great for conveying a sense of the culture (including, sometimes, the political culture) you are about to enter. Of course, they should not usually be relied on for topical analysis of recent political developments.

Our Malaysia researcher initially overestimated the dangers of his field research, which involved interviews especially with social movement activists. Describing himself as 'starting from zero', he discussed the risks of this fieldwork with various social scientists and a human rights activist about before going. He asked them what with hindsight seemed to him naïve questions: are activist leaders known by name, can you openly e-mail them? Nonetheless, he soon discovered that in Malaysia too, there are limits to how openly one can investigate anti-government protest.

The Iran researcher's preparations were very much colored by the events that had occurred towards the end of his PhD research: many of the activists he had interviewed and befriended had been forced into exile after the failure of Iran's Green Movement. Moreover, he had not returned for five years and had published critically on Iran in western media in the meantime. The advice he received from Iranian contacts was ambiguous. He went ahead with his visit, which turned out to be not very dangerous, but not very productive either, as we will elaborate in later chapters.

Because of the heightened security concerns, our Mexico researcher proceeded with his research in stages: starting in the capital and taking time to take advice from a relevant human rights organization, before proceeding to the more risky subnational context of Veracruz. When he arrived, both the human rights organization in the capital and the local representative of an international security consultancy were aware of his whereabouts and the nature of his research. This did not guarantee that nothing would happen. But it did mean that if there were an arrest, a threat, an assault, the local actors with the most appropriate local expertise, and with at least some clout, could immediately be involved.

Our repeat visitors, now country experts, all prepare in similar ways: they read local news and keep up their network, speaking to local friends and colleagues on a regular basis. In this regard, there is not a clear distinction between continually updating their substantive knowledge of the political developments and assessing the risks associated with the next fieldwork trip. Even our China researcher, born and bred in China, constantly updates her sense of the trends and patterns in how much space there is for social scientists to do their work. She talks to trusted friends and colleagues on Chinese social media, practicing her interview questions and honing her sense of what can be said to whom.

Going the Anthropologist Way

And yet, until you go you cannot really prepare. Our experience is that, for a first visit especially, it is best not to want too much, too soon. Take time to adjust to your environment. Read local papers; have some conversations with the proverbial taxi drivers. Take a language class. Exploratory talks are necessary, background conversations to orient oneself on what is safe for oneself and others. Visit your embassy, perhaps an international organization. Talk to some foreign journalists, some local academics.

More than in relatively democratic settings, authoritarian fieldwork requires caution, patience, and the willingness to accept that it is not always possible to interview those one wants to speak to, or ask them the questions one had planned to ask (see also Loyle 2016, 930–932; Malekzadeh 2016, 863–864; Markowitz 2016, 900–901 on creativity and flexibility in research design). The first few weeks, perhaps the entire first visit, may not yield immediate results. You have to go and see what is possible and slowly develop a plan to relate what you want to find out to what seems possible on the ground. In some contexts one can contact relative strangers via e-mail, but more often one depends on introductions from friends (see also Chap. 4). It is also important at this stage to shed assumptions that turn out to be oversimplifications, for instance, that demonstrations are either for or against the government, or that the general population is either apolitical or deeply political.

Generally, we try to keep multiple people aware of our whereabouts. Many of us have one or more trusted local contacts, who know what we are doing almost on a daily basis. We stay in frequent touch with parents or partners, and we make sure that people at home and in the fieldwork country have each other's contact details, so they can consult in case of an emergency. About once a week, we discuss our progress, strategy, and potential security risks, with a colleague at our home university.

Encountering the Security Apparatus

The need to take it slow, especially on a first visit, is illustrated by an early experience of our Malaysia researcher. In his first few days, he discovered that students or taxi drivers spoke much more openly about both the government and the main protest movement, Bersih, than he had expected. After five days in the country, an apparently golden opportunity fell into his lap: a protest was planned against a free trade agreement. Two local contacts thought it would probably be fine for him to attend the demonstration and talk to participants—although his own embassy advised against it. He prepared a short survey, online as well as on paper, and proceeded to the demonstration bright and early. After a brief chat with two youngsters who planned to demonstrate, he sat down on a bench with one of them and pulled his survey out. Within minutes, two bulky plainclothes security agents sat down next to him and demanded to see his papers. They asked whether he had a permit, told him repeatedly that they could not guarantee his security, demanded his passport and proceeded to photograph it. They then told him to go back to his hotel, where he stayed the rest of the day, abandoning his plans for the survey. Two reflections follow from this early encounter: if this protest had not come quite so soon after arrival, the researcher would probably have known to keep a lower profile during the demonstration. At the same time, he might have been less intimidated by the incident, and might have had the phone number of a lawyer on hand. On a repeat visit, he successfully attended a Bersih demonstration.

As a PhD student, our China researcher never considered what she might do if security agents would want to interview her. But as a postdoc in our project, after hearing that various Chinese scholars and some foreign scholars' Chinese students had been approached by the security services, for a 'cup of tea', she began to prepare, and make, a mental list of what to do in such a situation. Before the second fieldwork trip for our project, a Chinese colleague in China told her that he had been invited to meet two local security agents. After talking about his own research on China and the EU, they asked him questions about our funder, the ERC. According to the colleague, it was a civil meeting and he did not feel any sense of threat; they did not warn him or force him to do anything. The agents were curious about social science research in the west in general, but appeared to be to have two specific concerns. First, they wanted to understand whether the ERC was comparable to funding institutions (e.g. the Ford Foundation) that fund human rights activists and frequently touch the 'red lines' (see next chapter) of the Chinese government. Second, they wanted to understand the purpose and intentions of our project: why did we want to understand things about Chinese politics? Did we want to use our knowledge of China to instigate revolt against the Chinese Communist Party? Did we want to use the experience and lessons from the Arab spring and use social media for rebellion in China? It was clear that they were not worried about western social science research on

China in general, but concerned about certain topics that might be funded by 'suspicious' sponsors or touching 'red lines'. Such a 'friendly visit' to a third party, indicating that a research project has somehow gotten onto the radar of the security services, appears to fit with the experience of some researchers in the post-Soviet sphere (Gentile 2013, 430) as well as Malekzadeh's experience in Iran (2016, 872).

We contacted our advisors and various China scholars, western and local. Their and our assessment was that the inquiry into our project did not constitute an unacceptable risk to our China researcher. We did, however, think through likely questions that security agents might ask. The answers, we agreed, should be truthful, but have an apolitical slant (see Chap. 3). Just as Gentile (2013, 430) advises, politeness and diplomacy should be observed as much as possible, and in the best case, an interview might actually present 'an opportunity to clarify possible misunderstandings'. Only the identity of our researcher's respondents, and details of what they said, should be sacrosanct. As it turned out, her fieldwork was entirely uneventful. She received no invitation and did not notice any surveillance or intrusion at all.

Some of the risky situations we have experienced are not directly but indirectly related to the authoritarian context. Our Iran researcher underwent an incident of attempted extortion (which we will detail in Chap. 5), the motive of which may just have been personal gain, but the act was committed by a person connected to a security agency. Such a person may have, or at least feel they have, a higher degree of impunity in engaging in such behavior. Likewise, the risk of sexual harassment is something familiar to any solo-traveling female, but may take on a more menacing aspect when the agent is a state official in an authoritarian context. Our Morocco researcher had such an experience. She was invited by an official to a formal dinner where she could meet many relevant contacts, but he refused to give her the name of the restaurant and insisted instead that she should meet him for a drink at his place. Our researcher resolved the dilemma by pretending to accept, but a few minutes before they were supposed to meet, calling him to say that a previous appointment had lasted longer than expected and that she was too far away to make it to his home. Thus the official had no choice than to pick her up where she was and go directly to the restaurant. During the dinner, the official kept on filling her glass. Understanding what was happening, she realized that the last thing she wanted was to find herself alone with him in his car. A good tip to the waiter made it possible to have a taxi ready for her in front of the restaurant. Thus when he offered her a lift, it took her only few seconds to politely refuse and jump into her waiting taxi. The incident illustrates the particular interface between gender-based and authoritarian risk that female researchers may face. When in doubt, it may be wisest to sacrifice a spontaneous research opportunity if there is a clear risk of harassment. The episode also suggests, however, that for a researcher familiar with the context, some skillful navigation can make it possible to grasp the opportunity whilst staying safe.

Data Security Trade-Offs

We do not know to what extent any of us are under electronic surveillance from security institutions from authoritarian or indeed democratic states. In Chap. 5 we discuss our actual experiences with electronic surveillance; here we describe our preparations for it. We take it as given that, as Gentile puts it '(w)hen doing fieldwork in countries ruled by authoritarian regimes it is possible that phone calls, emails and letters are monitored', and further assume that any online activity, or documents on online servers or in virtual clouds, may be subject to scrutiny. Our most elaborate fieldwork preparations as a group related to data security, in particular contact details of respondents and interview transcripts. Before our fieldwork, our project had organized a few digital security training sessions from an expert in this area. With hindsight though, we have come to second-guess some of our initial learnings from these sessions, which were very much inspired by a post-Snowden focus on digital surveillance and online intrusions at the expense of thinking through more traditional security threats and basic travel precautions. One common device we had agreed on was to take two laptops into the field: one for web browsing, e-mails, and so on and one secondhand laptop that never went online, but acted almost as a typewriter, for transcribing interviews. We would keep these separate from the actual contact details of these respondents.

We have found, however, that applying high levels of digital security also has disadvantages. Now, we tend to think data security more in terms of trade-offs. The first is that it is simply time-consuming and cumbersome. In Kazakhstan, our researcher initially used two computers and two phones, with three SIM cards. Both the China and the Malaysia researchers took no less than three laptops into the field, a heavy load. Transcribing interviews on an offline laptop protects respondents from electronic surveillance and would make their identity hard to detect, but of course it does not offer absolute security. It also increases the chances of losing transcripts. Indeed, our researcher in Gujarat,

India had a terrible experience of this kind. Having done quite a few sensitive interviews with opponents of Narendra Modi, he had meticulously stuck to the strategy of keeping anonymized transcriptions only on the offline computer, and separately on USB sticks. On his trip back, transferring through Abu Dhabi airport, he kept both in his hand luggage. This bag was stolen—or possibly confiscated, we'll never know—*during baggage screening* at the airport. It was never recovered.

Another trade-off is that extreme security measures can actually draw suspicion. If you behave like a spy or *agent provocateur*, you are more likely to be suspected of being one. Our general policy has been to rely on the notion, accepted in most but perhaps not all authoritarian contexts, that social science research is a legitimate enterprise (see also Chap. 3), and we engage in it openly, but we have a professional duty to protect our data, and usually also the identity of our respondents. Indeed, our Iran researcher was advised against bringing a second laptop because it might raise suspicion, and decided not to bring one. Likewise, our Kazakhstan researcher gave up using the second laptop after a while. She came to the conclusion that, given that her research topic was not particularly sensitive, the risk of raising red flags during passport control by having a second laptop actually outweighed the benefits of better protection from electronic surveillance. A final trade-off relates to how taking digital security measures makes us feel, an issue we will return to in Chap. 5. Precautionary routines may increase our sense of comfort during stressful fieldwork, but it can also end up making us feel unnecessarily paranoid.

The lengths we went to protect respondent identities and transcripts depended in part on the sensitivity of the questions we were asking, and in part on what was considered appropriate in the context. Our Kazakhstan researcher used pseudonyms for her interviews with students who had been on a state-sponsored study-abroad scheme, but did not encrypt them. In Kazakhstan, the use of encryption is subject to legal restrictions, and would immediately signal that one has something to hide. Moreover, some experts believe that the introduction of a mandatory 'national security certificate' for Internet users in 2015 has actually made encryption more vulnerable to surveillance by the security services. Since her respondents came from a relatively select group of people, she thinks that if somebody would have gotten hold of her computer, they would surely have found a way to connect transcripts to respondents. However, she did not ask particularly sensitive questions, so if a state agent had somehow come to read or listen to the interviews, respondents would still not have been endangered. In the case of Malaysia, many of the activists interviewed were well-known public figures, who were comfortable going on record with everything they said, so there was no reason to keep the transcripts concealed offline, or separate them from names and contact details.

Our Iran expert by contrast, who has also interviewed activists, has taught himself to routinely use encryption. When he first started doing research in 2008, he had concerns about his transcripts getting physically impounded. However, he did not know much about Internet surveillance at the time, and he would simply e-mail his transcripts to his partner back home before erasing them. In 2015, he erased all data from his laptop before traveling to Iran. Less sensitive interviews he kept on his laptop, a bit hidden away with nondescript file names, more sensitive ones he would encrypt.

Some of us never record interviews but rely exclusively on extensive notes. Notes, they say, can have the advantage of making respondents more comfortable but also of making the interviewer more attentive to what she is hearing. Others do use recordings, but not for the most sensitive issues. All of us make copious notes, often in a mix of languages and even scripts, which are not readily intelligible to others. In case of extremely sensitive confidential information, we sometimes write nothing down at all but try to commit it to memory. There is an obvious tension here, which we will revisit in Chap. 6, between accuracy and transparency on the one hand, and protecting ourselves and our respondents on the other hand.

We went through a learning curve, from having little awareness of data security issues to assuming that rigorous measures like the use of offline laptops and encryption provide the most safety to thinking in terms of trade-offs between greater digital security on the one hand and the risks of arousing suspicion, physical theft, or becoming caught up in paranoia on the other hand. Our general experience has been that it is worthwhile to learn and practice a range of digital security routines before going into the field, so that we know how to use them if we find that the context requires it. If we then find that the routines we had envisaged are unnecessary or even inappropriate, we can relax or abandon them. The other way around, ratcheting up one's digital security routines once in the field, could be technically and practically much more difficult.

Chapter Conclusion: Planning Ahead and Accepting Risk

Preparing as well as we can may improve our judgment when faced with a sensitive situation, and—not unimportantly—give us some peace of mind. Ethics procedures, when well designed, can actually help us prepare by pushing us to think about challenges we might face. We prepare in advance by reading up from various sources, and by talking to politically minded people who live in our fieldwork country, or have visited recently. Visa procedures sometimes give us our first taste of the vagaries of authoritarian bureaucracies. We should take some time to acclimatize on arrival, especially if it is a first visit, the situation has changed, or our topic is particularly sensitive. We scenario-plan how we might handle an encounter with security agents. We can develop and practice digital routines. But even for experienced country experts, or people who are nationals of the state they investigate, unexpected situations may come up, and there is no fail-safe way to prepare and to figure out exactly what is and is not dangerous for oneself and others. Having assessed and minimized our risk, we accept that it exists.

References

Ahram, A. I., & Goode, J. P. (2016). Researching Authoritarianism in the Discipline of Democracy. *Social Science Quarterly, 97*, 834–849. https://doi.org/10.1111/ssqu.12340.

Central Eurasian Studies Society (CESS). (2016, March 5). *Taskforce on Fieldwork Safety.* Final Report. Retrieved July 19, 2017, from http://www.centraleurasia.org/assets/site/cess-task-force-on-fieldwork-safety_final-report-march-2016.pdf.

Clark, J. (2006). Field Research Methods in the Middle East. *PS: Political Science & Politics, 39*, 417–424. https://doi.org/10.1017/S1049096506060707.

Davenport, C., & Stam, A. C. (2009, October 7). What Really Happened in Rwanda? *Miller–McCune Research Essay.* Retrieved June 20, 2017, from https://psmag.com/social-justice/what-really-happened-in-rwanda-3432.

Gentile, M. (2013). Meeting the 'Organs': the Tacit Dilemma of Field Research in Authoritarian States. *Area, 45*, 426–432. https://doi.org/10.1111/area.12030.

Gladstone, R. (2017, July 17). Colleagues of Princeton University Scholar Convicted of Spying in Iran Express Shock. *New York Times.*

Goode, J. P. (2010). Redefining Russia: Hybrid Regimes, Fieldwork, and Russian Politics. *Perspectives on Politics, 8*, 1055–1075. https://doi.org/10.1017/S153759271000318X.

Goode, J. P. (2016). Eyes Wide Shut: Democratic Reversals, Scientific Closure, and the Study of Politics in Eurasia. *Social Science Quarterly, 97*, 876–893. https://doi.org/10.1111/ssqu.12343.

Goode, J. P., & Ahram, A. I. (2016). Special Issue Editors' Introduction: Observing Autocracies from the Ground Floor. *Social Science Quarterly, 97*, 823–833. https://doi.org/10.1111/ssqu.12339.

Kassam, A. (2016, October 10). Canadian-Iranian Professor: I Survived Imprisonment by Studying my Captors. *The Guardian.*

Loyle, C. E. (2016). Overcoming Research Obstacles in Hybrid Regimes: Lessons from Rwanda. *Social Science Quarterly*, *97*, 923–935. https://doi.org/10.1111/ssqu.12346.

Malekzadeh, S. (2016). Paranoia and Perspective, or How I Learned to Stop Worrying and Start Loving Research in the Islamic Republic of Iran. *Social Science Quarterly*, *97*, 862–875. https://doi.org/10.1111/ssqu.12342.

Markowitz, L. P. (2016). Scientific Closure and Research Strategies in Uzbekistan. *Social Science Quarterly*, *97*, 894–908. https://doi.org/10.1111/ssqu.12344.

Matelski, M. (2014). On Sensitivity and Secrecy: How Foreign Researchers and Their Local Contacts in Myanmar Deal with Risk Under Authoritarian Rule. *Journal of Burma Studies*, *18*, 59–82. https://doi.org/10.1353/jbs.2014.0008.

Pepinsky, T. (2017, January 6). *Everyday Authoritarianism Is Boring and Tolerable*. Retrieved July 21, 2017, from https://tompepinsky.com/2017/01/06/everyday-authoritarianism-is-boring-and-tolerable/.

Schreck, C. (2015, March 31). Western Scholars Alarmed by Russian Deportations, Fines. *Radio Free Europe/Radio Liberty*. Retrieved June 15, 2017, from https://www.rferl.org/a/russia-western-scholars-alarmed-deportations/26929921.html.

Wall, C., & Overton, J. (2006). Unethical Ethics?: Applying Research Ethics in Uzbekistan. *Development in Practice*, *16*, 62–67. www.jstor.org/stable/4029860.

CHAPTER 3

Learning the Red Lines

Abstract In this chapter we, as scholars of authoritarianism, discuss the 'red lines', a term used in authoritarian contexts to denote topics that are highly politically sensitive. We first describe commonalities in what the red lines are in different contexts, distinguishing between hard red lines and more fluid ones. We describe how we navigate red lines in fieldwork by offering a depoliticized, but not untrue, version of our research; how we adapt our wording and behavior to remain within the red lines, but still give us meaningful research results; and how we respond when the red lines shift, and words and behaviors previously acceptable become taboo, or vice versa.

Keywords Authoritarianism • Field research • Red lines • Sensitive topics

Observers of Chinese politics use the term 'red lines' to denote topics that are highly politically sensitive, the idea being that these are lines that must not be crossed. A red line does not necessarily mean that a topic cannot be discussed at all, but great care must be taken how it is discussed, and with whom. The term 'red lines' is also used in Morocco, and in Farsi there is also such an expression. In other contexts, we have not come across the phrase as such, but we adopt it here as a useful shorthand for topics or issues that are sensitive in the sense that investigating them is considered

M. Glasius et al., *Research, Ethics and Risk in the Authoritarian Field*,
https://doi.org/10.1007/978-3-319-68966-1_3

threatening or forbidden by the regime (see also Ahram and Goode 2016, 840). Thus, our notion of 'red lines' is distinctly political. We do not discuss primarily cultural dimensions of what constitutes appropriate or inappropriate topics and behaviors. Of course a field researcher also needs to be aware of cultural taboos but that is not a matter restricted to authoritarian contexts.

In this chapter, we first describe what we know of what the red lines are in different contexts. We distinguish between hard red lines and more fluid ones. With respect to the hard red lines, we find considerable commonalities across countries. For us as scholars of authoritarianism, understanding the red lines is our bread and butter, but we believe it is important for any professional visitor to an authoritarian-ruled state to at least gain an understanding of the hard red lines. The fluid lines are much more context-specific, more dependent on who we are interacting with, and more subject to change over time. The main commonality here is this ambiguity itself, which keeps us in uncertainty about precisely what is permissible.

We devote the bulk of the chapter to discussing how we navigate the red lines. Our primary strategy, and that of others, has been to be open and honest about the fact that we are social science researchers, and to explain the nature of our research in terms that are approximately accurate, but stripped of their politically sensitive import, so as to stay within the red lines. We give many examples, from our own experience and that of others, to elucidate what we mean by a 'depoliticized version' of our research, giving special attention to the wordings we use, and how local contacts can help us adapt our wording. We also give some examples of behaviors that, while far from being outrageous, came close to or crossed the red lines. Finally, we devote some attention to how the shifting of red lines over time can affect research.

Hard Red Lines

While the hard red lines are taboo subjects, it is not particularly difficult to discover, even before entering the field, what they are. What they have in common is that they are directly connected to regime stability, or the regime's core legitimizing narrative. In Iran, it is always the Supreme Leader: you cannot criticize him or question his position. In Morocco, likewise, his Majesty the King is a red line topic, and in Kazakhstan, it is the President who has been head of state for the last 28 years. In China, members of the Politburo Standing Committee can never be criticized.

Corruption is an important political topic in many of the contexts we investigate, and it is not necessarily controversial to discuss corruption as a societal problem. But investigating corruption in relation to the current top-level leadership is almost always taboo. This is true for the top leadership of the Chinese Communist Party and for the Iranian Revolutionary Guard. There is ample evidence of how sensitive investigating top-level corruption in authoritarian contexts is and of how regimes respond to it. An investigation by *The New York Times* journalists on the wealth of then Chinese prime minister Wen Jiabao's family resulted in the blocking of the newspaper's website in China (Barboza 2012; Branigan 2012). In Malaysia, a deputy public prosecutor was killed after investigating a corruption scandal in which the prime minister was embroiled, and allegedly leaking information about the case to the press (*Sarawak Report* 2015). In a decentralized country like Mexico, certain states are notorious for attacks on journalists who investigate the involvement of state-level officials in corruption scandals. None of us has done field research on the authoritarianism-corruption nexus, and we know relatively few academics who do so. A recent book that does focus on the nefarious financial networks of Central Asian leaders relies primarily on desk research (Cooley and Heathershaw 2017, 20–22), especially from court cases, leaked documents, and NGO sources.

Two other common red lines are ethnic or religious cleavages in society, and occupied or secessionist territories. These issues are red lines because openly discussing them can put into question the societal and/or territorial cohesion of the authoritarian state. In Malaysia, the 'special rights' of Malays in relation to primarily Chinese and Indian minorities are a red line and cannot be questioned. On the one hand the government exploits the fears and tensions between the different groups to some extent, positing itself as the guarantor of peaceful relations; on the other hand, it may genuinely fear large-scale ethnic unrest, as well as Islamic radicalism. In Kazakhstan discussing ethnic relations is problematic, unless framed in terms of the official discourse of harmony and tolerance. In China, focusing on conflicts between the Uyghur minority and other ethnic groups is unacceptable. In Rwanda, as reported by Loyle (2016, 925), asking questions about a person's ethnic identity is actually proscribed by law. Questioning Morocco's sovereignty over the Western Sahara, or suggesting that the rights of the local population are being violated, is a red line for Morocco, as is questioning whether Tibet or Taiwan belongs to China in the Chinese context (see also Reny 2016, 916).

Fluid Lines

Beyond the hard red lines, it is clear who is in power, but it is never certain what exactly is possible. As Loyle (2016, 924) writes about Rwanda, authoritarian regimes create 'a gray area around certain research topics. Restrictions are vague and punishments appear random. As a result, scholars may be unclear about what is or is not permitted and confused about the potential consequences of asking different types of research questions'. There is always a margin of error. Citizens of authoritarian countries, especially those who operate in political contexts, whether they are officials, critics, academics or students, corporate executives, or journalists, carefully assess their navigation of the fluid lines. If they cross them, even in a private, anonymous interview with a foreign scholar, they will not be doing so unwittingly. Local journalists in particular consider the red lines every day. For them, the lines are different, more restrictive, than for us, because what they write or say is read or heard by a broad local audience immediately, rather than by a narrow English-speaking academic audience, many months later. They can be a good source for us precisely because they may sometimes want to express to us privately what they know but cannot communicate openly in their own work.

A fluid line, for instance, is the degree to which government institutions and politicians below the leadership can be discussed and criticized. In Kazakhstan, there is some, and in China, Malaysia, and Morocco, even considerable leeway to critically discuss and investigate specific ministries, local authorities, or government policies. Intra-elite rivalries sometimes increase the space for sensitive research, but there can also be a danger of getting caught up in them: in Iran, for instance, contact with westerners can in itself be the subject of intra-elite mistrust and slander.

Likewise, there is great variation in the degree to which anti-governmental activism is sensitive. In Iran, the topic of political prisoners is a red line, as is the Green Movement to some extent. In Malaysia, the main protest movement campaigning for clean and fair elections, Bersih, operates quite openly. Today, while not everyone feels comfortable participating in the protests, discussing them is not experienced as problematic. But the religious and ethnically based anti-governmental Hindu movement ('HINDRAF') is much less openly tolerated and a more sensitive topic of discussion. In China too, the degree to which one can discuss protests publicly really depends on topic and context. Our China researcher found her online posting of information on protests in Hong Kong censored; but when she posted or forwarded international news coverage of a mass protest against a proposed factory in Northeast China, nothing was blocked. We can approach these differences analytically, thinking of reasons why a minority movement is more sensitive than a cross-ethnic movement, or why Hong Kong is more of a red line than a local protest in the far north, but we also believe that when it comes to the fluid lines, distinctions can be more arbitrary and do not always lend themselves to logical explanation.

Depoliticizing the Research

One of the clearest, most commonly agreed recommendations in the emerging literature on fieldwork in authoritarian circumstances is to 'frame the research topic in a way that has the best chance of reducing any sensitivity around it' (Art 2016, 980). This appears to be a common practice among scholars of the post-Soviet region, as reported in the Central Eurasian Studies Society's recent task force report on fieldwork safety. According to their survey, '(m)any respondents admitted to adjusting the presentation of their research topic to decrease risk. Some respondents indicated that they either do not disclose their real research topics to anyone or change how they describe their work depending on the context, whether a government institution, university, etc.' (CESS 2016, 6). The report also mentions that a 'small minority reports outright misrepresenting their purpose for being in-country, a practice that we [the taskforce] find ill-advised' (CESS 2016, 7) because of the risk it poses to local helpers after publication of the real research. Making research sound 'bland and gray', avoiding 'phrases that hint at political curiosity or other sensitive topics' (Turner 2013, 398) is apparently also a usual approach to field research in socialist East Asian states including China, Laos, and Vietnam (Cornet 2013; Petit 2013; Sowerwine 2013, all cited in Turner 2013; Reny 2016). Country specialists on Iran (Malekzadeh 2016), Kazakhstan (Gentile 2013), and Rwanda (Loyle 2016) all refer to similar strategies. While most accounts recommend depoliticizing research for pragmatic reasons such as gaining access and reducing risk, Malekzadeh (2016, 866) adds the important insight that an interest in the mundane may actually improve research validity. While initially 'looking for dramatic or expressed bursts of opposition or bouts of justice seeking under authoritarian rule', he learned instead to seek out 'how people negotiate with what can be a suffocatingly tedious and impenetrable bureaucratic setting in order to improve their own lives'. This chimes with Pepinsky's (2017) plea for attention, in the Malaysian context, to 'everyday authoritarianism' rather than looking for spectacular repression.

Just like these other scholars in the authoritarian field, we do not tell lies about what our research is about, and we do present our plans in ways that are neutral, non-specific, and depoliticized. But depoliticizing political science research is easier said than done. Below, we elaborate on our own practices and the examples given by others in order to give practical substance to what it means to 'make it boring' (Malekzadeh 2016, 865).

First, there is the term 'authoritarianism' itself. The common research project that we mainly draw on for this book is called 'authoritarianism in a global age'. It is no secret that we investigate authoritarianism. If you google any of us, you will come across the term, and it is likely that all our publications, some more prominently than others, will feature the term 'authoritarian'. In China, interestingly, authoritarianism itself is not a red line, or at least until recently it was not. Government officials do not themselves refer to the regime as authoritarian, but foreign and even domestic scholars openly do so in conversation, if not in Chinese publications. It is not considered a term of opprobrium, just an analytical distinction from democracy. In Morocco by contrast, where the regime likes to see itself described as 'democratizing', authoritarian as an adjective applied to the Kingdom is a red line.

But regardless, in explaining what we do during fieldwork, most of us never use it. It is not even that it would necessarily be dangerous to do so, it is just unhelpful. Speaking of authoritarianism (or democracy for that matter) invites abstract discussions about ideologies, cultural differences, or western hypocrisy. Some respondents might react badly to the suggestion that their government is authoritarian; others, especially activists, might actually embrace it. Either way such discussions often lead us away from the concrete things we want to find out. We might refer to the general project as being about comparing different state responses to globalization, and then go on to describe our specific research interest.

Our Chinese researcher when introducing herself, especially to officials, gives them her business card—which has her name and affiliation in Chinese and English, but not the name of our project (see also Loyle 2016, 929 and Malekzadeh 2016, 867 on business cards as symbols of the legitimacy of our status as researchers). She gives them many details, lots of answers to any questions they may have, so they are not left with the feeling that she is hiding anything. In her recent research on the interactions between Chinese companies and government agencies over big data, she would not mention concerns about privacy, surveillance, or censorship. Instead, she would refer to US companies and government-corporate relations to initiate conversations. Taking the United States both as a competitor and point of reference allowed government officials as well as company managers to talk easily about the Chinese situation.

Our Iran researcher, when interested in online censorship, surveillance, and harassment by the Iranian authorities, framed this as an interest in Iran's Internet policies, or recent developments regarding the Internet in Iran. Even in interviews with activists, he would not introduce the term 'censorship' into a conversation himself but follow the lead of a respondent in terms of the wording and the depth of discussion.

Loyle, in the context of Rwanda, also gives some very concrete examples of how to depoliticize research topics: 'it may be unwise (or prohibited) to ask questions about government corruption in distributing natural resource contracts but alternate wording of the research question, such as "contract allocation" or "indicators of governance effectiveness," can provide similar answers without drawing unwanted attention to your research. Concepts such as "state violence" or "repression" can easily be replaced with words such as "conflict" to suggest general patterns of violence instead of research directed toward abuses by the state' (Loyle 2016, 930).

Sometimes, with a particular type of respondents, we find that there are advantages to dropping the depoliticized version that we crafted. Our Malaysia researcher, after initially being cautious, discovered that much more could be discussed openly than he expected, and it worked to be very forthright. He began to introduce himself to activists as doing research on Internet and protests in authoritarian regimes—usually adding that it was debatable how authoritarian Malaysia was. This was also the experience of our researcher on the subnational contexts of India and Mexico. He found that using the word 'authoritarian', which is not exactly commonplace in these formally democratic states, was actually helpful when speaking to local opposition figures and journalists. These illustrations just go to show how context-dependent the appropriate ways and degrees of depoliticizing one's research are. In most other authoritarian contexts, such an opening would be most alarming to respondents and kill any chance of a good interview. But in these specific contexts, with this particular group of respondents, it was actually an icebreaker.

Wording

Knowing the red lines is not just a matter of knowing what can be discussed but also how to discuss it and with whom. In referring to the various heads of state above, we instinctively remained within the red lines: to refer to the Supreme Leader or his Majesty the King as plain Khamenei or Mohammad VI would be disrespectful. Not dangerous, but inappropriate and therefore unhelpful, especially in conversations with officials, but sometimes also with ordinary people. We have learned this by listening carefully, in formal and informal conversations, to how locals spoke of their leaders.

Just as there are appropriate and inappropriate forms for referring to the head of state, there may be commonly understood neutral terms for sensitive topics, as well as terms that raise alarm bells. Matelski found that in Myanmar before democratization, 'people often referred to "the situation" to describe the general conditions they had to live in under military rule without having to go into detail' (Matelski 2014, 64, 67). Many Iranians will refer to the Green Movement's large-scale post-election protests, and the subsequent regime repression of the movement, obliquely as 'the events of 2009'. Our Kazakhstan researcher found when she worked for the United Nations that, while many citizens engaged in what we would call volunteering, it was very difficult to find an acceptable vocabulary to talk about these activities. There are two words in Russian for 'volunteering'. The one with a Latin root (*volonterstvo*) was connected with the English-speaking world, foreign NGOs, and aid programs. People then reacted negatively to the notion of Kazakhstan as a third world country in need of foreign aid, and government accusations that foreign NGOs were 'importing' protest caused further suspicion. But her conversations fared no better with the other word for volunteering, which has a Slavic origin and was used in Soviet times for obligatory 'volunteering' for communist party-affiliated organs. How to talk about volunteering was not just a cultural or linguistic conundrum; it had political implications. From the government's perspective, the line between what is acceptable volunteering and what is not is very thin, revolving around the distinction between political and apolitical activities.

When speaking to officials, we sometimes adopt their discourse to some extent. Members of a constitutional reform commission in Morocco, for instance, were keen to describe the reform as a participatory process. Instead of questioning this, our researcher took up the notion of participation and asked to know more about who participated and how. Tailoring the wording of research to fit the preferences of respondents is not in itself unique: Art, for instance, described his research on radical right parties in Europe to party officials as an interest in parties 'very concerned with preserving the distinctive political and cultural values of their societies' (Art 2016, 981). What is distinctive about the authoritarian context in comparison is the element of risk involved (see Chap. 2), which can go well beyond being unfavorably received by potential respondents.

Getting Locals to Vet Your Wording

In case of doubt as to what wording of research questions may be more acceptable, while still conveying enough to elicit meaningful responses, the advice of trusted locals can be extremely helpful. When our Kazakhstan researcher first prepared for fieldwork, a diplomat turned researcher from the region helped her with the wording of letters to officials she wanted to interview, making the research sound harmless and interesting to them, and even flattering. Instead of asking after the authoritarian functions of the government party, he suggested she should ask officials how the party contributes to government effectiveness. Our Mexico researcher showed a human rights worker in the capital his list of proposed questions before traveling to the region, and was advised not to use the stark word 'repression', but speak of 'control' instead, or 'safeguarding information'. Reny describes the even more finely tailored advice she got from local collaborators in her research on underground churches in China. With pro-regime respondents, '(s)entences referring to house churches as "suppressed" (*bei yazhi*) or "controlled" (*bei kongzhi*) would automatically be replaced by "supervised" (*bei guanli*). These discursive subtleties would help reduce possibilities that interviewees interpreted my words as a critique' (Reny 2016, 919).

Having trusted local people consider one's wording is even more important when doing surveys. Contrary to what one might think, survey research is possible in authoritarian contexts—on some topics, in some countries. Three of us have conducted surveys. In survey research, one typically has no direct contact with one's respondents, no way of gauging their reactions and no chance to course correct. Surveys, moreover, leave an electronic or paper trail. Therefore, it is even more important than in face-to-face interviews to stay within the red lines, in terms of wording and topics. Our Malaysia researcher discovered that—while the political implications of ethnicity are in themselves a red line—it was considered crucial, in a telephone survey, that respondents were approached by interviewers of the same ethnicity, in their own language. Otherwise, he was told, respondents would not feel comfortable discussing political views or concerns at all. Our Kazakhstan researcher, despite extensive experience in the country, relied on local survey professionals to get her question about political activities phrased correctly. Our Chinese researcher ran her survey questions by some Chinese survey experts, and found that what she thought of as acceptable, neutral questions, relating to Chinese students' attitudes to democratic countries, or their views on the values of freedom or justice, could not be asked directly at all. The experts laughed and told her she had been abroad for too long.

Behaviors

While most of our advice about navigating red lines revolves around choice of words, other forms of behavior too may be shaped and constrained by the 'red lines'. In the authoritarian field, a course of action that would appear completely natural in a less constrained context may entail a risk of exposing self or respondents. In the Chinese context, Reny (2016, 919) describes taking public transport with two missionaries for whom it might have been better not to be seen with her: '(b)y the time we got there, I realized we should have taken a taxi instead. Not only were we in a suburb where locals were not accustomed to seeing foreigners, but also we had to walk 10 minutes on the main street to reach their apartment … (l)ocals on the street had enough time to notice me'. Our India researcher similarly found that he needed to course correct to avoid exposing respondents. Having gotten quite comfortable with the political setting after three months of fieldwork, he was conducting interviews in a coffee house well-known to be frequented by left-wing activists, and hence—but he was not aware of this at the time—also by government agents. After firing off some sensitive questions about the Maoist insurgency, he was warned by one of his interlocutors: 'if I were you I would ask your questions a little bit more discreetly'. No difficulties ensued for respondents either in the Chinese public transport incident reported by Reny or in the Indian coffee house, but as always in these contexts, we constantly need to reflect on our behavior, because there *might* be consequences.

Constant reflection on his own conduct, in relation to the 'red lines', was also the mode that our Malaysia researcher found himself in when attending an anti-government demonstration in 2016. Foreigners are not allowed to demonstrate, and his own embassy had advised against attending. Despite a bad experience during previous fieldwork (see Chap. 2), he decided, based on his own assessment and local advice, to go. During the demonstration he was continuously assessing whether to best be alone, or visibly part of a group; what he would do if anyone wanted to take a photo with him; what if anyone gave him the movement's yellow t-shirt to wear; what if the police would ask him what he was doing there. The demonstration, and his participation in it, passed without incident, but by the end of the day, he was exhausted by the constant self-assessment.

A very different fate befell Clotilde Reiss, a master's student who was in Isfahan, Iran, during the Green Movement protests in 2009, participated in the protests and took pictures, and apparently sent a brief report to the French research institute in Tehran (Ayad 2009). She was arrested and spent nearly a year in an Iranian prison. While our Iran researcher would think twice about giving information to western embassies and diplomats, especially by e-mail, reporting back to a research institute under these extraordinary circumstances is not a behavior beyond our comprehension. But in Iran, especially at that time, the accusation of 'spy' attached very easily to westerners, and she paid a heavy price. In terms of our behavior then, we sometimes walk a fine line between becoming overconfident and touching a red line, and being overcautious and sometimes a little paranoid. In Chap. 5 we will discuss the mental impact of such preoccupations in more detail.

Shifting Red Lines—Closures

The political fields we study do not stand still. Our China and our Kazakhstan researcher have both experienced that since they did their PhDs, there has come to be less scope for critical political discussion, whereas our Iran researcher has first witnessed a more liberal environment becoming very restricted and then again somewhat more relaxed in recent years. In China in recent years, the domestic academic climate has contracted. There used to be considerable leeway for—relatively abstract—discussions about political values, such as the meaning of citizenship or the value of democracy, in university classrooms. Currently, it appears to be the case—although it is difficult to verify conclusively—that students are encouraged to report about what teachers tell them in the classroom, a practice that has not occurred since the Cultural Revolution. This directly impacts on what can be done during fieldwork. Previously, the accessibility of information directly from policy-makers might fluctuate, but academics were always an easy source of comments and analysis. Nowadays, it is getting increasingly difficult to talk with officials even with appropriate introductions (see next chapter), and even the utterances of academics depend on longstanding relations of trust. In Kazakhstan, the red lines have not so much shifted as hardened. In the years 2007–2011, the authorities were trying really hard to open up the system to respond to the requests of international organizations (the OSCE in particular, of which they were trying to get the chairmanship for 2010), which did have a liberalizing effect. Nowadays, both online and offline media appear to be more controlled, and there is less tolerance of dissent. In the more factionalized political environment of Iran, the supreme leader was always a red line, but since 2009, the institutions that harbor political hardliners, the Revolutionary Guard and the judiciary, have also become more sensitive as topics.

Beyond our own experiences, it is important to recognize that, while there may usually be a correlation between increasing authoritarian practices in a particular country and conditions for field research becoming more challenging, the two trends are analytically distinct and do not always move together. The Central Asia task force cited in the previous chapter, for instance, writes that 'many respondents commented on the increasing authoritarianism in Azerbaijan, but the threat is much more acute for citizens of the country than for foreigners', and appears not to have had a direct impact on the research environment so far (CESS 2016, 7).

Shifting Red Lines—Openings

In transition contexts by contrast, researchers have had the experience of finding their customary caution suddenly unnecessary, and actually a hindrance. One of us, a regular visitor to Egypt in the 2000s, interviewed a range of activists in Cairo when Morsi was president. While the situation was volatile, she found respondents utterly unrestrained in what they said and where they said it. One took her to a famous graffiti wall in a busy street near Tahrir Square and began, in broad daylight, to interpret the political imagery, pointing and speaking. The wall has since been destroyed, and such behavior would again be unthinkable today. Analogously,

Matelski (2014, 72–73) relates how, working on civil society in Burma during the junta period, she had taught herself to speak in the idiom of oblique references that her respondents used. On a return visit after transition had been announced, she found that researchers new to the context 'did not seem as bothered by warnings and sensitivities and seemed able to discuss issues that I had been hesitant to bring up'. She attributed this discrepancy, not to 'oversensitivity on my part, or lack of context sensitivity on their part. It was simply the context that changed more quickly than any of us could have imagined'.

Chapter Conclusion: Navigating the Red Lines

We have tended to stay away from the hard red lines in our work on authoritarianism. We have been open about being political science researchers doing fieldwork. Perhaps there are circumstances in which it is both ethical and productive to act otherwise, but we find such circumstances difficult to imagine, and would be very reluctant to undertake 'undercover' research. Like others in the field, we do believe it is ethically justified, and mostly fruitful, to present our interests in a neutral and depoliticized light, as long as what we say is not beside the truth. We are professionals who have no sinister intent to destabilize the government. We present our research as analytically driven, perhaps a little technical and boring, and we strive to keep our behavior away from the red lines too. We typically err on the side of caution, especially in the early stages of our fieldwork, but sometimes find that we rapidly need to change gear to respond to unexpected openness.

References

Ahram, A. I., & Goode, J. P. (2016). Researching Authoritarianism in the Discipline of Democracy. *Social Science Quarterly, 97*, 834–849. https://doi.org/10.1111/ssqu.12340.

Art, D. (2016). Archivists and Adventurers: Research Strategies for Authoritarian Regimes of the Past and Present. *Social Science Quarterly, 97*, 974–990. https://doi.org/10.1111/ssqu.12348.

Ayad, C. (2009). Fin d'une longue captivite pour deux otages. *Liberation*. Retrieved July 20, 2017, from http://www.liberation.fr/planete/2009/11/27/fin-d-une-longue-captivite-pour-deux-otages_595967.

Barboza, D. (2012, November 24). Lobbying, a Windfall and a Leader's Family. *New York Times*. Retrieved July 20, 2017, from http://www.nytimes.

com/2012/11/25/business/chinese-insurers-regulatory-win-benefits-a-leaders-family.html.

Branigan, T. (2012, October 26). New York Times Blocked by China After Report on Wealth of Wen Jiabao's Family. *The Guardian*. Retrieved July 20, 2017, from https://www.theguardian.com/world/2012/oct/26/new-york-times-china-wen-jiabao.

Central Eurasian Studies Society (CESS). (2016, March 5). *Taskforce on Fieldwork Safety*. Final Report. Retrieved July 19, 2017, from http://www.centraleurasia.org/assets/site/cess-task-force-on-fieldwork-safety_final-report-march-2016.pdf.

Cooley, A., & Heathershaw, J. (2017). *Dictators Without Borders: Power and Money in Central Asia*. New Haven and London: Yale University Press.

Gentile, M. (2013). Meeting the 'Organs': The Tacit Dilemma of Field Research in Authoritarian States. *Area, 45*, 426–432. https://doi.org/10.1111/area.12030.

Loyle, C. E. (2016). Overcoming Research Obstacles in Hybrid Regimes: Lessons from Rwanda. *Social Science Quarterly, 97*, 923–935. https://doi.org/10.1111/ssqu.12346.

Malekzadeh, S. (2016). Paranoia and Perspective, or How I Learned to Stop Worrying and Start Loving Research in the Islamic Republic of Iran. *Social Science Quarterly, 97*, 862–875. https://doi.org/10.1111/ssqu.12342.

Matelski, M. (2014). On Sensitivity and Secrecy: How Foreign Researchers and Their Local Contacts in Myanmar Deal with Risk Under Authoritarian Rule. *Journal of Burma Studies, 18*, 59–82. https://doi.org/10.1353/jbs.2014.0008.

Pepinsky, T. (2017, January 6). *Everyday Authoritarianism Is Boring and Tolerable*. Retrieved July 21, 2017, from https://tompepinsky.com/2017/01/06/everyday-authoritarianism-is-boring-and-tolerable/.

Reny, M. (2016). Authoritarianism as a Research Constraint: Political Scientists in China. *Social Science Quarterly, 97*, 909–922. https://doi.org/10.1111/ssqu.12345.

Sarawak Report. (2015, November 25). *Kevin Morais Drew Up The Charge Sheet Against Najib And Later Leaked It To Sarawak Report, Says Brother*. Sarawak Report. Retrieved July 25, 2017, from http://www.sarawakreport.org/2015/11/kevin-morais-drew-up-the-charge-sheet-against-najib-and-then-sent-it-to-sarawak-report-says-brother/.

Turner, S. (2013). Red Stamps and Green Tea: Fieldwork Negotiations and Dilemmas in the Sino-Vietnamese Borderlands. *Area, 45*, 396–402. https://doi.org/10.1111/area.12017.

CHAPTER 4

Building and Maintaining Relations in the Field

Abstract In this chapter, we discuss the centrality of personal connections and trust in the authoritarian field. We consider our relations with local collaborators, the responsibility we have towards them, and the consideration of risk in such relations. We also discuss relations with interview respondents, the ways in which we approach them to try and maximize our chances of building trust, and how we 'work with what we have' in terms of our ascriptive characteristics, presenting a version of ourselves that helps us get information. We reflect on having been subject to manipulation by local contacts and respondents. Finally, we consider the debt we owe collaborators and respondents in the field, and the limited ways in which we can do something in return.

Keywords Authoritarianism • Field research • Trust • Research assistants • Respondents • Interviews

Societies everywhere run on social networks. Even in the Netherlands or in the United States, connections make social science research much easier. But in North West Europe and in Anglo-Saxon societies, networks may be a little less central than in most other societies, and it is sometimes possible, for instance, to get an elite interview based purely on a professionally worded e-mail and some follow-up phone calls. In non-western societies, networks of trust are typically much more important to everyday

M. Glasius et al., *Research, Ethics and Risk in the Authoritarian Field*,
https://doi.org/10.1007/978-3-319-68966-1_4

interactions, and getting meaningful information from strangers is much less likely. In authoritarian contexts, where the cost of having an even slightly politically loaded conversation can be high, trust and willingness to help come from who recommends you, and from how much effort you invest in assuring your respondent of your trustworthiness and respect for them.

In this chapter, we discuss how we have built our networks in the field and reflect on the centrality of personal connections and the currency of trust. We consider the relations we have with local collaborators, the responsibility we have towards them, and the (sometimes mutual) considerations of risk in such relations. Then, we hone in on one of the most important relations in authoritarian fieldwork: relations with potential interviewees, or as we will consistently call them in this chapter, respondents. We will discuss why interviews are often not refused outright, but evaded, in authoritarian contexts. We describe the ways in which we approach potential respondents to try and maximize our chances of building trust and discuss our experiences with encountering—and sometimes overcoming—three frequent obstacles to trust in authoritarian contexts: suspicion, ideological hostility, and fear. Our ascriptive characteristics (i.e. nationality, ethnic background, age, and gender) partly determine how we are perceived by respondents, but we describe how we 'work with what we have', presenting a version of ourselves that helps us build trust and get information. We explain how we navigate interviews with officials and activists, respectively, and reflect on a few cases where we have been subject to manipulation by local contacts and respondents. Finally, we consider the debt we owe collaborators and respondents in the field, and the limited ways in which we can do something in return.

Building Connections

We all come by our respondents via the 'snowball method', but a snowball is really the wrong metaphor, since it is the warmth of the connections that matters. People meet you, not necessarily because they are very interested in your research, but more because they trust you or the friends who introduced you to them. How warm these connections need to be depends on the kind of respondents, the topic, and the authoritarian context. In the least repressive context we work in, our Malaysia researcher found it relatively easy to meet activists who were public figures. The main concern was getting them to make time in their busy schedules. Talking to ordinary people who had occasionally attended demonstrations about their experiences was even easier. But even here, speaking to people who sympathized with the protests, but were for various reasons fearful of attending them, did really require personal introductions from their friends.

Practically, getting an introduction may just mean getting a phone number, but symbolically, it means much more. A certain capital of trust comes with the introduction. They take responsibility for us, providing a kind of safety check on behalf of their contact. In the experience of our China and our Kazakhstan researcher, a conversation with a potential respondent will almost always start with them getting a sense of the warmth of our connection with the liaison person: how do you know this person? How did you meet? For how long have you known each other? They may also try to discover whether anyone else in their circle is a friend of ours. According to a colleague of North African descent, someone with local roots may need even more time before the interview can start. Much more than in the case of a foreign researcher, the respondent needs to make a detailed assessment who is in front of him or her, and to what networks they belong. Are they linked to anyone in the regime or the opposition? These things will influence the extent to which the respondent will trust and help us.

Sometimes, the centrality of personal recommendations makes a respondent impatient with our habit of explaining our project and getting informed consent: a trusted person has vouched for us, the respondent feels, so let's skip the formalities and jump to the questions you have. They may express it in so many words: so and so is a friend, so tell me what I can do for you. Occasionally, an institutional contact may be a functional equivalent of a personal connection. Our Mexico researcher got various journalist contacts via a human rights organization, and found its name to be a magic word among potential respondents: it was the one organization they completely trusted. As always, there are exceptions to our rules, also to our 'networks are everything' axiom. One of our colleagues working in the Arab world has great experiences with going through secretaries or personal assistants to make appointments with officials. More than their bosses, they may be under the impression that we are 'important' because we come from abroad, and if they have a return favor to ask, it may be something small related to our knowledge of the western world.

In circumstances where being introduced by someone really means coming with their stamp of approval, contacts may not always be willing or able to make the introductions we desire. Our Iran researcher has experienced that people mention names of potential interview partners, but they may say ‘maybe it is not so helpful that I introduce you because there are differences, we have a different political orientation’. Or they will just say ‘it would be good for you to talk to this state secretary and I can give you his mobile number, but if you call him just like that it will not help you to get an interview’. Our China researcher has also come across such reluctance. Sometimes she is given contact details, but without the all-important personal introduction, sometimes they introduce her to another connection who could link her to the interviewee, and sometimes even after a potential interviewee has agreed to talk, they behave reluctantly: they reply to SMS very slowly or not at all, or remain evasive about a concrete meeting. It is not always possible to glean why our existing contacts are reluctant or unable to make forward introductions. It may just be that they are cultivating their own social capital carefully, and see a potential risk without advantage in making the connection for us, or it may be because the contact is not warm enough to successfully establish the connection. Or, as was most likely the case in Iran a few years ago, it is a sign of a contracting political climate and shifting alliances. Finally, there may be a gender dimension to a reluctance: some men may be considered inappropriate for a female researcher to meet, or vice versa.

When a local contact does make a connection for us, we may not fully know what goes on between them and the respondent. It may be that we unknowingly become an asset for the contact, who is trying to impress someone with their international network. Or the other way around, the respondent may extract something from the contact for having been exposed to us. It may not always be necessary to fully understand what exchange is going on, but we should at least be aware of the possibility that either we or our contact are being put in an awkward position of owing someone a favor, especially if the interview does not in fact go well.

There is a tension, in authoritarian contexts, between the need to rely on local contacts and snowball sampling and the need to be discrete about who our interviewees are (see also Ahram and Goode 2016, 843). When we rely on local contacts and respondents to provide us with further contacts, it is quite natural for them to be asking who else we are speaking to or have interviewed. In some contexts, giving this information may be entirely innocuous, but in other cases who we speak to may actually be sensitive information that might get respondents into trouble. It may not always be possible or appropriate to be entirely silent about interviewees while soliciting further contacts, but discretion can be exercised, especially about names we think might be sensitive, unless our local contacts are trusted friends. In general, a policy of openness should not extend to telling respondents details about each other.

Local Collaborators

Sometimes, ontacts may do much more for us than just act as go-betweens. Both our Morocco and our Iran researcher nowadays rely on a few people they know well, who will not only share contact details but help assess who will be useful to talk to, whether they are easy or difficult to approach, and whether approaching them might have consequences for the rest of our research, making it better to meet them towards the end of their stay. They also give their advice on security issues, on wording, or on how to interpret some initial impressions.

Some of these people come to work with us on a more sustained basis, because they are interested in learning social science methods, because they want to put their work for us on their CV, because they are simply curious or willing to help, or because they have become friends. Others are paid by us, as research assistants, translators, survey experts, or local supervisors. Mostly, the relationship is beneficial to both sides. Our Kazakhstan and Malaysia researchers have both had great experiences working with local survey companies, the staff of which were very skilled and professional as well as genuinely interested in the research projects in question. The Kazakhstan researcher also worked successfully with paid research assistants. Apart from simply saving time, she finds that they can help with wording things appropriately (see Chap. 3) and have their own networks and knowledge that facilitates the accessing of information. Apart from payment, she has helped them by discussing and commenting on their PhD theses or job applications. The seniority relation was the other way around when our India researcher did his first fieldwork: in accordance with the customary procedure in his master's program, he had a paid local supervisor. This payment allowed him to make use of the local academic's contacts, and use him as a sounding board, without feeling that the relationship was exploitative (see Carapico 2014, 27–28 on the sometimes shameless imposition by foreign scholars on local researchers). Since then, he has had occasional help with translating, both in India and Mexico, from people his own age who offered their help, and for whom he has paid travel expenses but no fees. He has been reluctant to pay these people, whom he considers as friends and stays in touch with. In China, students typically get paid for research assistance to foreign scholars, but also see it as an important opportunity for research training and experience. Our China researcher has used an assistant once, to find and interview a few people in Cantonese. Payment would have been considered offensive since this was a friend of a friend who volunteered to help, but our researcher wrote her a reference letter for study abroad in return.

The relationship with local collaborators can raise ethical concerns, however, when local collaborators are either inexperienced, or dependent on us, or both. Inexperienced collaborators, especially people with no social science or advocacy background, may not be fully aware of the possible risks connected with the collaboration. Even collaborators who are aware of the risks might agree to do more than it is safe for them because they feel a sense of obligation, either in the name of friendship and collaboration, or because they are being paid. Our Kazakhstan researcher felt greatly responsible, for instance, for volunteers who undertook a door-to-door survey for her and a colleague, something that is not very usual in Kazakhstan, and can make the police nervous. They took all the measures they could think of to make sure the volunteers were safe, gave them security training, passed on advice from professional survey-takers, and provided them with letters on university letterhead, stating that the researchers took sole responsibility for the survey in case they were stopped by the police, and so on. The survey was taken without incident.

Our general view is that we bear responsibility for research tasks undertaken for us, whether paid or not. While relying to some extent on our local collaborators' judgment, we also need to make our own assessment of whether what we are asking is safe for them to undertake, being aware that their position is different from ours because they have to continue to live and work in the country, while we can leave. Most of us feel that we can undertake such risk assessment, and working with local collaborators is a valuable way to save time, get the benefit of a local interpretation, and get access to additional material and networks.

While the greater concern should be whether our research causes risk to local collaborators, we should also be aware of the opposite possibility, that a local collaborator's other activities and local status compromise our research. As Hilhorst et al. (2016, 19) write 'researchers also need to consider the social position of their local colleagues, such as co-researchers, translators and drivers. If these people are controversial, the researcher will become controversial as a consequence'. Collaborators can get into trouble, not because of their research assistance to us but for other reasons. Our Morocco researcher recently paid a local collaborator she had known for a decade, for what was meant to be joint research. She did not hesitate about hiring him because he was a journalist known to be critical of the regime, and the work he would do for her was innocuous by comparison to his own publications. After showing her some initial work, he dropped out of contact for almost a year. She never discovered exactly why, but given the authoritarian context there is always the possibility that he may have received some sort of warning that caused him to cease all political activities. Having also had a complicated experience with undertaking dangerous research herself at the beginning of her career (see next chapter), she is now quite reluctant to work with research assistants, because of the risks on both sides of the relation, and would only consider the possibility if she were to start afresh in a new country with no contacts. Even those of us who do sometimes rely on research assistance still undertake the bulk of interviews ourselves. Below we describe how we go about our interviews in the authoritarian field.

Refusals

Even with introductions, chasing respondents for appointments is probably the most arduous aspect of fieldwork, and failure is not unusual. It happens that a potential respondent simply says no. Our India researcher once had a former rebel leader initially agree to an interview, but then later sending a text message simply stating 'I don't think this interview is in my benefit'. And our Iran researcher once found that a journalist and media scholar categorically refused to speak to him about a specific topic, despite the best possible introductions, because he found the topic too sensitive. But such frank, point-blank refusals are extremely rare.

For cultural as well as political reasons, the much more common experience is that respondents will agree to meet in principle but invent a series of excuses to make it practically impossible. Our Kazakhstan researcher experienced this while trying to speak to Kazakhstani students in the United Kingdom. She introduced herself to local university Kazakh societies and met apparently willing respondents there, but then when she tried to follow up, they were sick, they were busy, they had class, until she had left town. This may have been because she lacked the right introductions, or because she did not have enough time to follow up the group meetings with more informal personal chats to gradually build trust, or possibly because being abroad actually made the students feel more under the radar of the government than they would have been at home.

Our Chinese researcher has had quite a few such experiences, especially with policy-makers: they are busy, not in town, not in the office. One eventually agreed, after being pursued for a month and a half, to speak by phone, but then went silent completely, no longer replying to SMS messages. Another, after many e-mail reminders, asked to see a list of questions in advance, and then never responded. In some cases, this may be to do with the sensitivity of the topic. But in certain contexts, in our experience especially in China and Iran, meeting someone from a foreign university may in itself already be considered sensitive, whatever the subject, especially for officials. Such meetings may not pose an immediate risk to them, but they are on a career ladder, and meeting researchers may be held against them at some point. They are just trying to avoid doing anything that could be construed as wrong.

Testing the Waters

When meeting our respondents, we do not get straight to the point. Instead, we invest time in building the relationship, discussing health, families, traffic, and mutual acquaintances if possible. Sometimes this just takes the first few minutes of a meeting, especially when people are busy and used to being interviewed; at other times the entire first meeting is devoted to testing each other out. Sometimes, interviewees will not engage in a first meeting without the presence of the people who introduced us to each other, and only afterwards make an appointment for the second time. Thomson et al. (2013, 6), who work in the Great Lakes region of Africa, explain why so much effort needs to be invested in building trust: '(a)s researchers we cannot expect people to respond to us with openness, nor expect that they will tell us their real opinions and experiences when they have just met us. This is equally true for someone in a high-ranking government or rebel position as it is for someone in a remote rural area or someone meeting you in the centre of town. Why would anyone divulge sensitive information, that if known beyond the confines of your interview could get them into trouble with neighbours and local authorities alike?'

Knowing the local language is usually not an absolute necessity, but it can be an important asset, since most people are simply more comfortable in their mother tongue. Our Iran researcher believes that respondents are more open with him speaking Farsi, in part because they appreciate his knowledge of the language and in part because it makes interviews feel less official. But for others, the choice of language can have complicated political connotations, especially for researchers of local or dual heritage. Like our own Morocco researcher, a colleague of Moroccan descent who has grown up in Europe conducts interviews in French or English. This is not because he has difficulty speaking the local dialect of Arabic, but because his accent would lead a respondent to make immediate assumptions regarding his family's regional background and social class. His fluent English and French and prestigious academic affiliations can offset this, but in turn cause him to be seen as more of an outsider. By contrast, a colleague of Turkish descent who has spent most of his adult life in Europe finds that his accent gives him easy access to elite circles, but can cause him to be distrusted by ordinary Turks, and even more, Kurds. He prefers to use English in his engagement with Kurds in Europe.

Even when we get started with the real interview, there is always an initial part where you try to measure each other. As researchers, we try to assess how much we can push, not starting right out with the big questions. If we feel that there is a difficulty with a particular question, we may skip it and return to it later. Not all of this is about political sensitivities: not everyone is used to giving concise, to-the-point answers even to straightforward questions, and multiple approaches may be needed to get a question understood and answered. But when sensitive topics are being broached, it is all the more important to engage in a careful ritual dance. Showing up like a newshound, pen in hand and firing off questions will alienate even well-disposed respondents.

We have all experienced situations in which establishing trust was unusually difficult. We will illustrate three of the four most common reasons, as we have encountered them: suspicion, ideological hostility, fear, and personality. An example of suspicion was experienced recently by our China researcher, who was exposed to a kind of reverse interview by a policy-maker. For half an hour, she was asked directly and indirectly what she wanted, why she does this kind of research, why foreigners are interested in the details of Chinese policy-making, why our project got a big grant, what the EU's interest in providing such grants might be, and so on. Testing her patience, she must have given the desired answers, for she eventually got her interview.

In the survey of Middle East scholars undertaken by Clark (2006, 418), '(t)wenty-seven percent of researchers specifically identified anti-westernism (usually in the form of anti-Americanism) and the general suspicion and distrust of U.S. policies and perceived agendas as impeding their efforts to undertake field research' (see also Carapico 2014, 27; Jourdan 2013). We have not been as pervasively exposed to ideological hostility to westerners as an obstacle in field research as Clark reports, perhaps because we are not US nationals, and have mostly worked in European universities, but we have also come across it. Our Morocco researcher got used to always having to sit through a lecture on how Islam is not against women before being able to ask Islamist political actors the questions she was actually interested in. She once got a more than usually hostile reaction from a female Islamist activist, who attributed a question she did not like to the researcher's 'Judeo-Christian culture', and ended the meeting soon afterward, despite the researcher's protestations that her interest in the reform of Morocco's Family Law had nothing to do with her personal background. Our Kazakhstan researcher experienced ideological hostility in a spontaneous encounter with young party officials. After being briefly introduced by her contact, an intern, she was left to introduce herself. As soon as she started explaining that she was a PhD student in political science from Italy, a young man started talking about western scholars who go around criticizing other countries while neglecting the study of their political problems at home. He kept standing and declaiming these 'truths' in a loud voice and accusatory tone. While it was an unpleasant experience, and it made any actual interviews impossible, the incident could be considered as 'relevant data' in her research on the party's role in the authoritarian governance of Kazakhstan. Other encounters she and local researchers had with young party cadres confirmed that this aggressive way of arguing is something at least some youth branch leaders use against pro-democracy organizations or activists, to delegitimize their claims as something foreign, alien, and potentially destabilizing harmony in society.

Fear of reprisals nearly caused an intriguing interview for our Mexico researcher to be aborted: he had an initial chat via a mutual friend with someone who had an incredible story of state corruption—the building she had worked in was partly destroyed supposedly due to a gas explosion, but as an engineer who worked in the building she knew there to be no gas pipes in or under the building, and suspected self-sabotage. The respondent's indignation may have sparked her to initially tell the story, but she went on to cancel the planned second meeting in which she would discuss the incident in more detail, because she feared repercussions. Eventually, on a second fieldwork trip, and after another informal meeting, she opened up and told the full story. Fear was the main obstacle to getting interviews with civil society organizations in Burma under the military junta, undertaken by Matelski. She found that organizations that had no regular contact with westerners were reluctant to meet her, and even those that did 'remained reluctant to share information', as 'it could raise suspicion of secret dealings with journalists or activists' (Matelski 2014, 68–69). When we come across fear, we may try to put a potential respondent at ease, but it behooves us not to push too hard but to respect their judgment as to whether meeting us may pose risks for them.

Our experiences of respondents' suspicion, ideological hostility and fear all relate directly to the authoritarian context. But respondents in authoritarian circumstances are also just people, who can be stand-offish, overbearing, offensive, or dishonest for no particular reason. Sometimes, we just do not succeed in establishing a connection at a human level, and our interview experience remains frustrating. And sometimes, the 'click' occurs precisely when we give up hope and stop trying to fish for information. Our China researcher pursued a well-connected local scholar for over a month, only to be harangued for fifteen minutes about how 'out of date' and 'pointless' her research was. Just when she was ready to give up and leave, the scholar unexpectedly said that she could try to arrange a meeting with a significant insider. She followed through, and the subsequent interview turned out to be quite important. Our India researcher experienced something similar when interviewing a supporter of the Maoist movement in India: not getting substantive answers to questions, he let go and allowed the interview to turn into a free-floating conversation about historic revolutionary trajectories, to which he contributed his own reflections. Somehow, these ideas enthused the respondent, and he started sharing precisely the personal information on his own motivations that he had previously been holding back. These are just two examples of a common experience, that when we relax because the interview, whether frustrating or fruitful, is over, our respondent also relaxes and shares something with us that turns out to be more meaningful than anything we had heard from them before. Markowitz (2016, 904) actually recommends ending an interview with a 'concluding ritual', such as 'putting a pen cap on the pen and putting the pen on my notebook', precisely because it 'proved to be remarkably useful in relaxing informants and often they began a "side point" or "one more thing"'. Formally ending an interview but then asking 'just one minor question' is also advised by Art, who refers to Inspector Columbo in the classic TV series as the master of this stratagem (Art 2016, 981).

Work with What You Have

We think of relations with respondents as a kind of role-play: we do not pretend to be anything other than ourselves, but we do present particular versions of ourselves that we think will help us build the relation, and establish the best possible connection with our respondents. There are widely different strategies for this, which have a little bit to do with one's personality, but actually more with how we are seen by others on the basis of ascriptive categories like nationality, age, and gender. Below, we set out some opposites to illustrate how different characteristics propel us towards different roles—but these are stylized foils. In reality, our interviewer persona is not so entirely fixed: it may evolve over time, it partly depends on the type of respondent, and sometimes we may even change gear in the midst of an interview to get more traction.

Our researcher in India and Mexico, a young man doing research on forms of repression, typically tries to make the relation with respondents as informal as possible, often meeting people multiple times, looking for ways to break the ice, trying to make it 'click'. This approach seems quite natural when meeting journalists or human rights activists, who often have values similar to our own. But he has also applied it with 'agents of repression': police or security officials. One of his most revealing interviews has been with a security agent in a bar, who was detailing how he harasses opposition politicians for a living, while drinking and using cocaine. For our Morocco researcher, a young woman operating in the Arab world, such an approach would be a recipe for disaster: diving into informality with a relative stranger, seeking repeat meetings, being in places where alcohol or drugs are consumed could all lead to misunderstandings. Instead, she stresses her professional persona, makes it clear that interviewing people is 'work', and while engaging in the necessary small talk as described above, she deflects questions about her private life. Our Kazakhstan researcher, operating in a context less marked by stereotypical views about the sexual morality of western women, steers an in-between course. She would not meet respondents at a bar or in the evening, but her approach is a little more informal. She uses her nationality, making assumptions about respondent impressions of Italian culture, and emphasizing similarities like the importance of hospitality, late dinners, and big weddings.

Akin to the informal/professional divide, but a little different, is the choice to present ourselves as well-informed or naïve. Naivety is a commonly used interview strategy (Goode 2011; Solinger 2006; Henrion-Douncy 2013), typically more available to young women and foreigners. Our China researcher, while not actually foreign, uses both elements, especially with older men in senior positions (whether in government, research institutions, or companies) who often possess both stereotypical views of young women and valuable information. When it comes to gender, the experiences of other China scholars we know include one that illustrates our sense that women are considered less threatening, and may sometimes have greater access to officials precisely in authoritarian circumstances: two foreign researchers both did research regarding the top leadership of the party (i.e. the most sensitive kind there is, see our previous chapter) at roughly the same time. Both were given permission to do fieldwork, but when the male academic approached government officials, many people refused to speak to him. When the female researcher did, it was all green lights.

Apart from her gender, our China researcher also employs her partial outsider status, playing up the fact that she has been abroad for very long, which makes it possible for her to ask some relatively more sensitive questions that foreigners can usually ask, but that would not be available to a scholar who has remained in China. But she can switch from 'naïve' to 'professional', showing her familiarity with relevant details, when she feels that a respondent is spinning her a line. As we already illustrated in relation to the use of language, there is great variation in the positionality, and strategies available to, researchers with local or non-western roots (see also Malekzadeh 2016, 867). A colleague of Moroccan origin finds that he can only feign naivety to a certain extent. It would seem disingenuous to act as if he does not understand how things work in Morocco, and sometimes even when he is really baffled, locals still expect him to understand. Yom on the other hand, an American Middle East scholar of Korean descent, often found himself inexplicably cast as more of an outsider to the field than white western academics, and hence considered either more ignorant or more objective than they are (Yom 2014, 18).

In contrast to the naïve stance, showing that you have 'done your homework' has been the strategy of our Malaysia researcher when approaching well-known activists, who are typically very busy, sometimes a little self-important, and in regular demand for interviews with researchers and journalists. Display of expertise worked for him, for instance, with an activist who had been elusive and eventually told him to come and meet outside a bar where he was drinking with friends. The respondent initially took a rather abusive tone in front of his friends. Our researcher immediately launched into a detailed question about events twenty years ago, which eventually led to an in-depth one-to-one conversation and a follow-up at the respondent's home. In line with her professional persona, our Morocco researcher, who interviews mainly officials, similarly prefers to set out her 'case knowledge' of a topic early on so as to be taken seriously. She also builds trust by showing that she knows what she is doing in procedural terms, for instance, discussing the status of the conversation as off-the-record, anonymous, and so on. But she has also experienced how, working as a pair with a researcher less steeped in local knowledge, they managed to have it both ways, using expertise and naivety in tandem. Her colleague, who had a more basic command of French, could at some point break into the interview, posing quasi-ingenuous questions that she herself did not feel able to ask, but the boldness of which could be attributed to her inability to express herself more subtly in French.

A final consideration is whether to present ourselves as an 'important' or a very junior person. Again, our choices are very much constrained by age, gender, and position, but each of us can work with what they have. A male middle-aged full professor may well find it easier to get an appointment with an official than a young female PhD student. But by being considered more consequential, he may also be more threatening and may have less fruitful interviews. While our Morocco researcher regularly uses her doctoral title to get in the door, our Iran researcher by contrast still sometimes introduces himself as 'a student' to diminish his importance, years after finishing his PhD.

Where to Meet

We generally like to leave it up to the respondent to suggest a venue for meeting, but again there is a considerable gender divide, almost regardless of the context. Our Iran, Malaysia, and India-Mexico researchers are all male and interview primarily activists and journalists. For them, cafés, bars, and shopping malls are obvious meeting places. All of them have also occasionally met respondents at their homes. The women among us by contrast will avoid meeting strangers at their homes, at a hotel, or late at night. Beyond the gender issue, meeting a respondent in a public place implies that neither they nor we are uncomfortable about being seen together. This fits with our general commitment to being open about what we do, and not behaving like spies. Both our China and our Iran researcher have experienced that whether one meets in a café or restaurant or in someone's office may affect the flavor of an interview. Going to people's offices implies that the interview becomes more official, they will consider you more as a professional, and they use more official language; at a dinner people will be more relaxed and talkative. Going out to dinner does mean being seen together, possibly also by government agents, but both in China and Iran, people who are concerned about being associated with us would probably refuse a meeting in any case. Dinners with our liaison or others present are in a way also less political. Reny (2016, 918) describes, also in the Chinese context, how she was once refused an interview by an official, and given the message that the contact person 'should have invited him out to dinner' and then have the researcher join, so the meeting could have been presented as spontaneous. Dinner meetings do pose challenges for note-taking or recording however: neither are very practical or appropriate while eating food, so the researcher must somehow rely on her memory and write it all up immediately afterward.

Triangulation, Not Confrontation

While we have very different approaches to how we present ourselves and where we meet, we have considerable consensus on what to avoid during an interview: confrontation. Confrontation is a frequently employed style of interviewing in journalism. We do not know to what extent academic researchers in democratic circumstances ever employ confrontation as an interviewing strategy, but we do know that for researchers of authoritarianism, it is not a helpful approach to improving our understanding of how things work. It is not our job to influence the views of our interviewees, let alone change them, but to try and establish how they see things, or at least how they choose to present them. Our approach is markedly different in this respect from the one recommended by Markowitz (2016, 905), who writes that in authoritarian circumstances, interviewers 'need to be prepared to raise hard questions that bring tension into the room, to challenge informants when they are giving the official line and not their own viewpoint, and to identify discrepancies even to the point of calling him/her out on a false statement'.

There are two elements to our stance. First, while we are obviously critical in many ways of the political systems we study, we do not arrogate to ourselves the right to prescribe to the locals how they could be improved. The western societies we belong to or have chosen to live in are also flawed. Moreover, they may be directly or indirectly implicated, today and through a shared global history of exploitation and domination, in the authoritarian rule of the societies we study. The second reason is more pragmatic: confrontation is simply not productive to our line of work. It can lead to respondents shutting us out and spouting well-worn ideological positions rather than answering questions.

That is not to say that we swallow whole everything respondents tell us. Regardless who we speak to, we always assume it is their perspective, informed by their worldview, and often their interest, that we get. Our job is not to push back during the interview—at least not aggressively—but rather to place it in context based on triangulation with other sources. While there is great variation in how much interesting information respondents have, how much they want to share, and how well they can remember and tell us, there is no such thing as a bad interview. There is always something worthwhile about every encounter, even if it was not at all what we were looking for, and never makes it into our written work, it still adds to our overall understanding of things.

We are undoubtedly more at ease speaking to like-minded people, that is, people who in some way have a critical stance vis-à-vis the regimes they live under, than speaking to zealous or bureaucratic government officials. We quickly establish a friendly connection based on shared understandings, and they may be happy to encounter someone they can have an open conversation with. There is a risk here though, perhaps more than when we speak to officials, of bias. Spending a lot of time with people who may already be closer to our worldview than many of their compatriots, we are likely to be influenced by their ideas, views, and discourse (see also Ahram and Goode 2016, 843). At the same time, being more similar to us than others does not always make them the most interesting respondents. In fact, some of us have the experience that people who see themselves as intellectuals can be difficult interviewees, because they like to speak in abstract terms and share their entire worldview, when we are looking to hear factual details, or personal experiences. We have also found activist views to be sometimes marked by vanity and bravado, at other times by excessive cynicism about their role, or by a predilection for conspiracy theories (to which we find authoritarian settings generally conducive).

In interviews with officials, we approach people with respect, knowing that just as we are doing our job, they are doing theirs. Even if somebody is literally telling us lies, we will not openly contradict them. This would only humiliate and alienate them. Instead, we treat their version of the truth as interesting. To give an example, our Kazakhstan reporter interviewed the director of an NGO. She knew from other sources that his was not a 'real' NGO but an organization reliant on state funding, without significant grassroots support. Instead of challenging him about the absence of a popular constituency, she asked him more neutrally about the organization's collaboration with state agencies in its activities, more gently exploring with him why and how he chose to present his organization as an NGO, what its actual status was, and getting answers.

Sensitive Information

Having made successful efforts to gain the trust of respondents, we will often be entrusted with sensitive information. While we take every possible care to keep our transcripts safe (see Chaps. 2 and 6), we cannot give an absolute guarantee that it will never fall into the wrong hands. In this context, we typically trust our respondents to make their own judgments about the information they entrust to us. We assume that they consider what they want to share with us, and that they are aware that there may be some risk in speaking to us, however minimal. We do this in the knowledge that their judgment is not infallible, but ours would not necessarily be better. Some will err on the side of caution. Indeed, our Morocco researcher once had a respondent spell it out in so many words when she asked him about the religious legitimacy of the King: 'if you can assure me that you can protect me I will give you my answer, I will tell you what I think—but since you cannot I will not answer your question'. Others may be less forthright but make the same call.

Our general experience with officials is that they are very much aware of exactly what they can and cannot say, they are used to weighing their words, and they will rarely be reckless. The experience with activists is a little more varied. On the one hand, they move in a complicated political setting, and we know they think about this a lot. On the other hand, they would not be activists in an authoritarian setting if they were entirely risk averse. Sometimes they can be too nonchalant, or too much affected by a stranger's interest in hearing their views and experiences. Our India and Mexico researcher has had the experience that a respondent instantly began sharing some quite inflammatory information without making much effort to properly understand who was interviewing him, for what purpose, and with what safeguards. In such a case, we might reconsider whether it is actually responsible to use the information we have been given, whereas when we feel that the respondent has carefully considered what they have told us on the record, we will have fewer qualms (see also Chap. 6 on how we write up and reference our sources).

Being Manipulated

As described above, we assume that respondents have a particular version of the truth that they want to share with us, perhaps even an agenda, and while it can be challenging to figure out how to value and triangulate different accounts, we consider this part and parcel of our craft. But occasionally, we have encountered more blatant forms of manipulation. It is easy to suggest in the abstract that one should not fall for such attempts, but in practice it can, for different reasons, be difficult to avoid being manipulated. We describe a few of our experiences and try to draw some lessons.

One such pitfall is the 'resentful respondent', who may have valuable information to share, but has his own reasons (resentment against the system in general, or against a particular person) to speak to us. On one level, such a person can give us access to information that we would otherwise not be able to get. However, precisely because such data cannot easily be triangulated, it is more than usually difficult to assess its veracity. A second risk is that, unless we can keep the contact entirely confidential, it may interfere with the willingness of others to trust and speak to us. Both our India and our Kazakhstan researcher have encountered a 'resentful respondent'. Whereas the India researcher has cultivated the contact while being aware of the risk of manipulation, the Kazakhstan researcher decided to forego the opportunity. The difference lay not so much in their ability to judge the veracity of the respondent's account, as in their research topic, and the associated opportunity cost: the Kazakhstan researcher feared it would interfere with the relationship she was building with other party cadres, whereas the India researcher was already focusing on regime critics rather than insiders, so had little to lose.

Our Iran researcher has experienced the opposite situation: being manipulated by a former dissident turned regime informer. He met this young journalist, who wrote about films and had reformist leanings, on his first visit to Iran, spent time with him regularly, and developed a friendship. On a return visit, the journalist told our researcher he had been arrested before and feared another arrest. He instructed our researcher that if he should drop out of contact, the researcher was to deliver a prewritten press release reporting the journalist's renewed arrest to Reporters Without

Borders and other advocacy organizations. When the journalist did in fact disappear, our Iran researcher, concerned for the fate of his friend, did indeed send the press release. It later transpired that this second arrest was fake. During the first arrest, the journalist had been put under pressure and had become an informant for the intelligence agency. The pretend second arrest was intended to dispel suspicion among the fellow government critics on whom he was informing. With hindsight, our researcher believes he should have discussed the situation with other contacts before sending out the press release. If he had done so, he might have picked up on rumors already circulating that this person was an informer, and he would have reconsidered sending the press release. But it was precisely the authoritarian context that caused him to be secretive and trust no one.

A third instance of manipulation, experienced again by our Kazakhstan researcher, involved her being invited to write (a very minor piece of) propaganda for the regime. At the time, Almaty was bidding to host the 2022 winter Olympics, a bid eventually won by Beijing. A warm contact, a young official she had known for many years, and had seen rise in various government positions, called with a small request. She was asked to write an English-language article (in fact she was sent a suggested text but told she was free to write whatever she liked) for a website about what a nice city Almaty was, so that the local media could in turn quote this foreigner's piece supporting the bid. Despite the fact that the article did not need to be overtly political, and might have been published on an obscure website, she decided that writing it would compromise her integrity as a scholar. But there was a price to pay. She attempted to limit the offense to her contact by citing her team leader's prohibition as the reason, but her refusal nonetheless did irreparable damage to her relationship with a very helpful contact.

Since every situation of manipulation is different, it is difficult to draw general lessons. The last of the three incidents sketched here is perhaps the easiest to adjudicate: what we do for a living is write, and one of the reasons our writings are valued by society is their independence. We do not necessarily take a 'neutral' stance, but straightforward advocacy either for or against the regime interferes fundamentally with our ability to form and disseminate autonomous views. For the other situations, an important suggestion is not to act precipitously, and to recognize that you do not have to be all alone in making these judgment calls. A decision taken after reflection and consultation both with trusted local contacts and academic colleagues at home (without unnecessarily divulging sensitive details) may be a better decision, even when we do not have as much information as we would like on which to base it.

Doing Things in Return

There are different reasons why respondents are willing to talk to us. At the simplest level, it is because we ask them, and most people like granting a polite request better than refusing it. Some respondents feel under an obligation to the people who introduced us. Many have an agenda of some sort, which may be their own or that of the organization they represent. Government officials may be flattered that their views and experiences are deemed relevant to scientific research, considering it a boon to their personal prestige to be interviewed by a foreign researcher. Activists are often just happy that there is one person more who knows what they are doing. Without the willingness of all sorts of people to speak to us, share their time, their views and their knowledge with us, we would not be able to do our work. The same is not true for them. We may occasionally be in a position to do a respondent a favor, but overall, we cannot be as crucially useful to them as they are to us. This puts us in their debt. We try to handle that debt as best we can.

This begins with recognizing the debt, showing appreciation, and signaling our willingness to do something in return. As Loyle (2016, 933) puts it, 'acknowledging a basic responsibility to contribute in some small way goes far in demonstrating respect for the individuals who give of their own time for our research'. At the simplest level, after a good conversation, we can send a respondent a message to thank them. If we promise to share results with respondents, in the form of a published article, then we would normally need to keep that promise. But making such a promise and keeping it is not always possible, either simply because respondents may not be able to read English, or, more specific to the authoritarian context, it might be problematic for them to receive the text. One of us conducted interviews with activists in Cairo during the Morsi period, and intended to send them her findings, but by the time the research was published, the situation in Egypt had changed so dramatically that she did not think it safe to send them the report or subsequent articles.

We try to stay in touch with respondents after the interview but it does not always happen; we are busy and perhaps they are too. While we will acknowledge our sources, they often need to be anonymized, and sometimes their contribution to our understanding needs to be downplayed for their safety (see also Chap. 6), making our acknowledgment appear inadequate. Our Iran researcher, for instance, ended up not acknowledging his Iranian tutor in his PhD thesis, published during the most restrictive period after the Green Movement in 2012. Likewise, the research assistant and translator on the Cairo interviews mentioned above was never acknowledged by name.

When it actually comes to returning favors, there are often—very contextual—cultural as well as ethical constraints on what is appropriate. Our local academic contacts we can sometimes repay very appropriately, by offering to teach a class to their students. Even if we are wary about teaching political science topics because they might be sensitive, we might teach on our home country's politics, and there is always methods teaching. Some of us may be able to teach quantitative methods, but most likely, we have expertise in qualitative methods, such as interviewing and document analysis, which is a topic under-taught at most western universities, let alone non-western ones. At other times, we may be helpful to respondents by helping them navigate forms or websites or write in English. But we also need to be clear about what is not possible: we *can* help respondents fill out applications for visa or scholarships, but we *cannot* help them get the visa or scholarship.

We often meet respondents in cafés or restaurants. From a research ethics perspective, we all consider it entirely appropriate that we should offer to pay the bill. We see it as a token of appreciation, not as any kind of remuneration. However, we have found that cultural norms are widely divergent on this matter, and unintended offense may be given if we get it wrong. In China, paying is completely acceptable: after all you have invited the person, however senior they might be. Our Morocco researcher also frequently pays for a meal, and in fact finds the offer of lunch or dinner to be a useful response to officials who say they are too busy to meet during office hours. But our Kazakhstan and Iranian researchers' experience is that most respondents would be deeply offended by a paying researcher, taking it as a refusal of hospitality by a guest in their country. Students might be more willing to be treated, but even they might at least make a show of attempting to pick up the bill. Our Malaysia researcher found that, while he paid for drinks for ordinary young people as a matter of course, activists were adamant about paying for themselves for a different reason. Possibly because of government allegations regarding foreign funding, they had a heightened sensitivity towards accepting even the smallest thing that might be construed as a bribe. When it comes to small gifts, our practices also diverge. Most of us might bring presents for personal friends to our fieldwork, but not for people we meet for an interview; but in China, a bookmark or some tea, worth less than 5 euros, is quite acceptable.

None of us ever pay for interviews. We can imagine circumstances in which it might be appropriate to do so: with respondents who are particularly poor and vulnerable, to the point that recording their material hardship without doing anything to alleviate it would be unethical. This might make sense, for instance, when interviewing undocumented migrants, people in IDP camps, or slum dwellers. But our own research has not typically focused on the most marginalized. In the authoritarian field, we believe payment poses various problems. First of all, any significant sum would cause a power shift: the respondent goes from being a 'creditor', giving us their time and insights, to being in our debt. This might cause them to feel pressured to answer even when they are not comfortable to do so. Second, it can lead to 'desirable' answers, with respondents telling us what they think we want to hear, causing validity problems. Finally, in some contexts, payment would be considered suspicious by the authorities. This could pose risk to the respondents as well as delegitimize critical findings (see also Loyle 2016, 933, who lists the same ethical and validity problems with paying respondents in authoritarian circumstances).

More of a conundrum is posed by interviews with respondents from non-governmental organizations. Since they represent causes beyond their own self-interest, they can be quite forward about requesting a 'voluntary' donation in exchange for their time. The ethical implications of complying with such requests depend a great deal on the circumstances: it may be less problematic when we interview staff than when the organization acts as a gatekeeper vis-à-vis members or beneficiaries we would like to interview, and less problematic when solicited after an interview than before it. We have sporadically made such donations but emphasized that these were personal contributions to a cause we valued, not a form of payment, and indeed we have not expensed them. More often, we try to fend off such requests without giving offense, saying we will think it over.

Chapter Conclusion: Patience, Trust, and Recognition

Building relations with respondents for primarily interview-based research is not fundamentally different in authoritarian contexts than in politically open societies. In all cases, it requires social intelligence: fine-tuned antennae for the words and body language of people we interact with, and the ability to interpret and respond to these signals. It is just that, in authoritarian contexts, the need for these skills is further accentuated. Building trust is both more difficult and more crucial. Getting to the nub of what we really want to know requires more patience. As we have shown in this chapter, it is useful to reflect explicitly on our relation with our respondents, in both directions. This is even more so with local collaborators, where we must think through consequences of their possible dependence on us, especially in relation to risk. In interviewing, we have to find a balance between openness and presenting a persona that contributes to a constructive conversation. We also have to be accepting of the versions of the truth, some more plausible than others, that respondents share with us, and treat them as interesting and worthy of respect as well as in need of triangulation and critical analysis. While we are occasionally at risk of blatant manipulation, the more common situation is that we are indebted to our respondents, a debt that we acknowledge, but cannot fully repay.

References

Ahram, A. I., & Goode, J. P. (2016). Researching Authoritarianism in the Discipline of Democracy. *Social Science Quarterly, 97*(2016), 834–849. https://doi.org/10.1111/ssqu.12340.

Art, D. (2016). Archivists and Adventurers: Research Strategies for Authoritarian Regimes of the Past and Present. *Social Science Quarterly, 97*, 974–990. https://doi.org/10.1111/ssqu.12348.

Carapico, S. (2014). On the Moral Hazards of Field Research in Middle East Politics. In *The Ethics of Research in the Middle East.* POMEPS Studies Washington, DC: George Washington University (Vol. 8, pp. 27–29).

Clark, J. (2006). Field Research Methods in the Middle East. *PS: Political Science & Politics, 39*, 417–424. https://doi.org/10.1017/S1049096506060707.

Goode, J. (2011). Eyes Wide Shut: Democratic Reversals, Scientific Closure, and Post-Soviet Eurasia'. 9 Comparative. *Democratization, 2*(1), 9–13.

Henrion-Douncy, I. (2013). Easier in Exile? Comparative Observations on Doing Research Among Tibetans in Lhasa and Dharamsala. In S. Turner (Ed.), *Red Stamps and Gold Stars. Fieldwork Dilemmas in Upland Socialist Asia* (pp. 201–219). Toronto: UBC Press.

Hilhorst, D., Hodgson, L., Jansen, B., & Mena, R. (2016). *Security Guidelines for Field Research in Complex, Remote and Hazardous Places.* The Hague: ISS-EUR. Retrieved from https://www.iss.nl/news_events/iss_news/detail_news/news/5486-security-guidelines-for-researchers/.

Jourdan, L. (2013). From Humanitarian to Anthropologist: Writing at the Margins of Ethnographic Research in the Democratic Republic of Congo. In S. Thomson, A. Ansoms, & J. Murison (Eds.), *Emotional and Ethical Challenges for Field Research in Africa: The Story Behind the Findings* (pp. 12–27). London: Palgrave Macmillan.

Loyle, C. E. (2016). Overcoming Research Obstacles in Hybrid Regimes: Lessons from Rwanda. *Social Science Quarterly, 97*, 923–935. https://doi.org/10.1111/ssqu.12346.

Malekzadeh, S. (2016). Paranoia and Perspective, or How I Learned to Stop Worrying and Start Loving Research in the Islamic Republic of Iran. *Social Science Quarterly, 97*, 862–875. https://doi.org/10.1111/ssqu.12342.

Markowitz, L. P. (2016). Scientific Closure and Research Strategies in Uzbekistan. *Social Science Quarterly, 97*, 894–908. https://doi.org/10.1111/ssqu.12344.

Matelski, M. (2014). On Sensitivity and Secrecy: How Foreign Researchers and Their Local Contacts in Myanmar Deal with Risk under Authoritarian Rule. *Journal of Burma Studies, 18*, 59–82. https://doi.org/10.1353/jbs.2014.0008.

Reny, M. (2016). Authoritarianism as a Research Constraint: Political Scientists in China. *Social Science Quarterly, 97*, 909–922. https://doi.org/10.1111/ssqu.12345.

Solinger, D. (2006). Interviewing Chinese People: From High-level Officials to the Unemployed. In M. Heimer & S. Thøgersen (Eds.), *Doing Fieldwork in China* (pp. 110–129). Copenhagen: NIAS Press.

Thomson, S., Ansoms, A., & Murison, J. (2013). Introduction: Why Stories Behind the Findings? In S. Thomson, A. Ansoms, & J. Murison (Eds.), *Emotional and Ethical Challenges for Field Research in Africa: The Story Behind the Findings* (pp. 1–12). London: Palgrave Macmillan.

Yom, S. L. (2014). Why Race Matters. In *The Ethics of Research in the Middle East*. POMEPS Studies Washington, DC: George Washington University (Vol. 8, pp. 17–18).

CHAPTER 5

Mental Impact

Abstract In this chapter, we describe our encounters with targeted surveillance and intimidation, betrayal, and being confronted with hard stories of suffering, torture, and brutal murder. We consider the feelings of stress, fear, and paranoia that may result from operating in a repressive environment and what we need to do, individually and institutionally, to mitigate and manage the harmful mental impact of fieldwork. We then turn to how pressure to get results, and a sense of shame and career worries associated with not getting them, can compound negative impact of fieldwork. Finally though, we also record the positive effects of fieldwork on our psyche and worldview. We conclude with the importance of making it possible to talk about mental impact, before, during, and after fieldwork.

Keywords Authoritarianism • Field research • Surveillance • Stress • Trauma • Career pressure

In this chapter, we will discuss a topic that we believe receives too little attention: the mental impact that being in the authoritarian field has on us. As in earlier chapters, we focus on the specificities of the authoritarian field while recognizing that some of our observations may well apply to other kinds of 'difficult' contexts too. We all experience fieldwork as times of excitement as well as stress. Being away from our home life, in the presence of some risk, and having to process things very quickly, is tiring but

M. Glasius et al., *Research, Ethics and Risk in the Authoritarian Field*,
https://doi.org/10.1007/978-3-319-68966-1_5

at the same time gives us a lot of energy, because we get a lot of input. What is common to all kinds of fieldwork, and stressful in itself, is that we try to gather as much information and speak to as many relevant people as possible, always in a limited time. We often worry about whether we have done enough, and have the sense that we can always do more. For first-time researchers, an especially big question looms: will people talk to me at all?

Also common to all fieldwork far away from home, is our need to adjust to a context very different to our own. This extends to seemingly mundane problems like pollution and traffic, that can nonetheless have a considerable impact on our state of mind. Then there is the social and cultural adjustment. Even our China researcher, who is ostensibly visiting 'home', finds herself marveling at the hierarchy in the workplace and in the family, the way people treat each other in the street, and getting irritated by value differences even in conversations with friends. Our Iran researcher finds many of his close contacts depressed by the political and economic obstacles they face, and in turn he finds their inability to realize their potential depressing.

As researchers in authoritarian contexts, we probably face more refusals and less openness than other researchers. This can come in the form of avoiding an interview, as described in the last chapter. Even when we do get the interview, especially with officials, we are always playing a game, where we do not cross the red lines, but skirt around the edges, trying to draw out as much information as we can. Our obstacles can also relate to documents that we know exist, but that our respondents do not want to share with us, perhaps because their bosses will not give permission, or more generally because it is better in authoritarian bureaucracies not to take such initiatives. As a result, we can feel frustrated, knowing the information is there but we cannot get it (see Barros 2016, 964–965, on bureaucratic secrecy in authoritarian contexts). And while, as we have stressed before, authoritarian contexts are not unsafe for foreign researchers most of the time, they are marked by persistent uncertainty. We never know precisely what the regime knows and thinks of us and under what circumstances it might abruptly conclude that what we are doing is causing them a problem.

Below, we describe our encounters with targeted surveillance and intimidation, and the feelings of stress, fear, and paranoia that we have experienced as a result of operating in a repressive environment. We discuss the impact of either direct betrayal by, or a sense of disenchantment with, people we had cordial relations with in the field, and the impact of being confronted with hard stories of suffering, torture, and brutal murder, in the field or afterward. We consider the underdeveloped topic of what we need to do, individually and institutionally, to mitigate and manage the consequences of harmful mental impact of fieldwork: making mental impact a subject that can be discussed and made subject to a range of coping strategies; reflecting on the effects of stressful incidents and hard stories on validity and bias of our research; reconsidering after such events what fields, what subjects, and research questions we still can and want to investigate; and the physical impact of mental stress. We then turn to a broader issue in academia that can compound negative mental impact and complicate the usual mitigation strategies: the pressure to get results and the sense of shame and career worries associated with not getting them. Finally though, we also record the positive effects of fieldwork on our psyche and worldview. We conclude by emphasizing how helpful we have found sharing our fears and dilemmas. By doing so we hope to counter the academic predilection for focusing on achievements over discussing doubts and difficulties.

Targeted Surveillance

Since the Snowden revelations, the idea that our transactions, communications, and even our documents may be monitored and analyzed by unseen entities without our knowledge or permission has turned from an outlandish conspiracy theory into an open possibility for most Internet users worldwide. Interestingly, we find that this seems to be making us rather stoical about the possibility of being under electronic surveillance from the authoritarian regimes we investigate. Since our overall policy is to be open about the work we do, we do not encrypt or hide away our documents, other than transcripts or respondent contact details, as described in the last chapter. Drafts of this book, for instance, have been edited and saved on various servers and clouds.

Our China and Kazakhstan researchers have never personally noticed signs of surveillance. They are cautious about contact with vulnerable respondents online, but mostly the idea of surveillance remains rather abstract and does not affect them. The Kazakhstan researcher used to work in a formerly government-owned building that was commonly believed to be wired, but did not really care, nor did her coworkers. The China researcher has noted how quickly her Chinese acquaintances adapt, and develop language online that is mutually understood, but not picked up or blocked by automated censorship devices. She found that many of her interviewees happily contacted her via social media in the knowledge that there might be surveillance.

Our attitudes change when we get concrete indications that, rather than just being absorbed into general surveillance and censorship practices, we are specifically being targeted by security agents. Our Morocco researcher is certain that she was under electronic surveillance during one particular fieldwork period. Returning to her hotel after an interview, she opened her laptop and saw that her Google mail account had been accessed while she was out. She also received phishing e-mails that would appear to fit with what Moroccan activists and journalists have reported (Privacy International 2015). She has not had indications of electronic surveillance on subsequent field trips, but she is convinced that her phone is tapped when she is in Morocco and is careful about what she says on the phone. It took her time to come to terms with this. By repeating to herself that the people undertaking the surveillance were only doing their job, as she was doing hers, she regained her peace of mind. The electronic surveillance episode to her mind has validated her approach of taking handwritten notes rather than recording interviews (see ch.6).

Our Malaysia researcher does not have similarly definitive evidence, but both activists and ordinary Malaysians have told him that they assumed the authorities were reading his e-mail and WhatsApp messages during his field research. The activists he interviewed were fairly certain that they were being monitored: after they had agreed via WhatsApp to meet each other at a particular coffee house, special branch people would typically be seen at the coffee house at the appointed time. Initially our researcher was shocked to hear this and very cautious in his questioning. On reflection, however, he decided that if asked during an interview what he was doing, he would stick to our policy of openness and not lie but simply explain that he was conducting an interview. His respondents did not appear particularly intimidated, and for himself, he later thought, eviction was the worst thing that was likely to happen. One of the Mexico researcher's respondents similarly told him during an interview that phone conversations were tapped, and it was likely that security agents knew that the interview was taking place. As we will detail below, they had much more reason to be afraid than their Malaysian counterparts. Our Iran researcher similarly suspects that when he met journalists in their newspaper offices, these buildings were under surveillance, and notes may have been taken to document his visit. Giving in to this thought could make him feel somewhat paranoid from time to time, but he decided not to be deterred by a mere suspicion of surveillance.

In these cases, it remains ambiguous how pervasive the surveillance effort was, and also whether regime agents wanted us to know they were monitoring us, or tried to be subtle. While there may be exceptions, we should assume that in an authoritarian context, critical journalists and activists are likely to be under (online and/or offline) surveillance to some degree, and there is a good possibility that we as researchers may come under the radar if we contact them, even if we never notice it. None of this was ambiguous when our Morocco researcher was investigating human rights abuses committed against—real or supposed—Salafists. Soon after her meeting with relatives of Salafi prisoners (detailed below), she was conducting an interview in an otherwise empty coffee house, and two people came to sit at the next table, pretending to read a newspaper but clearly listening in to the interview. During the next two days, she was continually being followed. A man sat down next to her in a nearly empty train. She moved to another seat, but again she was followed. When she got out of the train, he was still there. When she arrived at the airport, the same person was in the queue behind her, but then magically appeared in front of her after security control. This was surveillance intended to intimidate, and it did.

For reasons detailed below, the Morocco researcher nevertheless returned to Morocco, but this time prepared a number of safety measures, making arrangements to meet friends at the airport, informing the Italian embassy of what she was doing, and asking for official permission to do the research. Faced again with intrusive surveillance, she met a friend at a coffee bar and, again with a security agent in a nearly empty café as audience, told her friend that she had no interest in the Salafi research; she was just doing it because she needed the money, her real interest was in women's rights. When for months her request for authorization remained 'in process', she acted according to her own stated intentions, and gave up the research on Salafists. She experienced some more surveillance, but as it became increasingly clear that she was no longer following this line of inquiry, the surveillance melted away. She had encountered a red line (see Chap.3) and has chosen not to cross it again.

Stress, Fear, and Paranoia

Most of the time when we are doing fieldwork, we are not afraid, we feel comfortable in the environment in which we are staying. Indeed, it would be impossible to do our work, staying in the field for weeks and sometimes months, if it were otherwise. But we want to come out and say that sometimes, when doing research in the authoritarian field, we feel anxious, afraid, even a little paranoid.

For some of us, the most frightening incidents have been those where we were directly targeted, such as the intrusive surveillance experienced by our Morocco researcher, described above. Our Malaysia researcher was quite frightened after the incident, described in Chap. 2, in which plainclothes police had photographed his passport. It was at this same time he discovered that his e-mail was probably being read. Moreover, the incident occurred within weeks of the death of Giulio Regeni, and the Dutch embassy had helpfully told him that a Dutch person was sometimes arrested and held for weeks without the embassy being informed—possibly to deter him from attending the demonstration. He spent a sleepless night expecting a knock on the door, and for the next few days continually considered the possibility of being arrested. After a few days, when nothing happened, he recovered his calm and continued his fieldwork uneventfully.

Our Iran researcher has experienced a terrifying incident with a much longer tail. In Chap. 4, we described how he had been tricked by a former journalist turned informer into corroborating this man's fake arrest, so as to bolster his cover. A year later, the same man (whom our researcher still believed to be his friend) showed up at his apartment, admitting that he worked for the security services and claiming that these had become very suspicious of the researcher. The man, whom we shall call Ramin here, could help close the file, but he needed money. Ramin then announced that 'one of my colleagues will enter your apartment also and he will search your apartment, but I will protect you.' Indeed, a second man came, and our researcher really panicked. Ramin wanted 4000 or 5000 euro, while the second person started searching the researcher's wastepaper basket and computer, finding handwritten notes about the arrest of bloggers and some saved articles by an Iranian French scholar, about whom they proceeded to interrogate him, closing the curtains of the apartment. They tried to get him off-balance.

He felt a mix of panic and amusement, because the situation was scary but also somewhat ridiculous, with both men behaving like movie script intelligence agents or interrogators. He remembers repeatedly thinking 'come on, now you are overdoing it' as the incident unfolded. Eventually, they allowed him to call someone, ostensibly to get the money. He called a friend, who could tell from his voice that he was very scared, and immediately called the French research institute with which he was affiliated. Eventually someone from the French embassy came to the apartment and took our researcher with him, to safety. Soon after, he left the country for a few weeks, in part for his safety, but especially also to calm down. In this case, it remains unclear whether the primary purpose of the plot was to steal money or to induce fear, but it certainly had that latter effect.

In overtly repressive contexts, we may also experience moments of fear that have nothing to do with us personally. Our Mexico researcher has been vividly aware during his field research of certain locations that have been the scene of horrific events. Coming to a shopping center for an interview, he experienced mental images of what had happened there a year earlier: a truck full of dead bodies had been dumped in the street. Another source of temporary bouts of fear or discomfort for him were the federal police at every street corner. Not only were they heavily armed, they are known to have been involved in various political murders.

As we have stressed in Chap. 2, instances of intimidation of foreign researchers are relatively rare. But they happen just often enough, in the broader context of what we know of the repressive side of the regime, to make us always a little apprehensive during fieldwork. As Malekzadeh (2016, 868) has related in the context of Iran, the likelihood was that he would not be in any danger, but he 'could not be certain why agents had checked up on me or where it would lead. The problem, of course, was the uncertainty. Regimes like the Islamic Republic excel in sowing doubt'. It is quite clear who is in power, but there is always a residual uncertainty about what we are allowed to do, and what can happen to us.

Betrayal and Disenchantment

The emotional response of our Iran researcher to the intrusion into his flat and subsequent extortion attempt was not just one of fear. He also felt a sense of betrayal. When he had first come to know Ramin, he had come to consider him not just as a respondent but also as a friend, who had helped him understand the political context of Iran and whom he trusted. When he sent out the press release about the man's supposed arrest, he had been concerned for Ramin's safety. When the intrusion occurred, he came to understand, from one moment to the next, that this was not his friend, this was someone doing him harm. He had difficulty believing that this was really true. But the sense of betrayal described here is not just personal betrayal, it has to be understood in its authoritarian context. As it happens, our Iran researcher grew up in East Germany and thought that his youth had taught him always to be suspicious. Instead, he had been too trustful and forgotten how ugly the intrusion of an authoritarian regime in personal relations can become.

Also characteristic of authoritarian circumstances is the lack of clarity, until this day, about the exact nature of the incident. Our researcher filed a complaint with the police, and it became clear that the police was not involved—they were furious and considered the incident as a criminal act. Nor does Ramin appear to have been working for the ministry of intelligence: an Iranian lawyer made some informal inquiries and found that there was no file on our researcher. Later it transpired that Ramin had been involved in the arrest of bloggers and journalists; in the following years, he became an editorial writer for the hardline conservative press. But it remains unclear whether, at the time of the incident, he had been connected to any of the various parallel intelligence agencies and whether the incident was just a brazen attempt at extortion, or at least in part a political warning.

Without being personally betrayed as our Iran researcher was, others also have the experience of seeing people whom they believed to be idealistic turn into regime apologists. Our Morocco researcher spent quite some time with journalists who used to criticize the regime but now work for pro-government media. She is careful not to judge them: these people were young when she met them and may at some point have decided in favor of having a family and a normal life. The price of being a regime critic can be very high, and we might make the same calculation in their position.

Our Kazakhstan researcher's experience with a rising government official over the last decade is slightly different: this man was never a democrat, but he had previously been a believer in 'changing things from the inside' as well as a warm personal contact. The more he progressed in his career, the more his attitude toward our researcher became distant and bureaucratic, culminating in a meeting where he put on display the perks of office, keeping her waiting for a long time, and then having her ushered in by an aide and served tea by a secretary. This was the same person who asked her to write a propaganda story for the Almaty Olympics bid (see Chap. 4). After her refusal, the relationship has cooled, and she would no longer ask him for contacts or other work-related favors.

Hard Stories

Many of us have spoken to respondents who have been in prison and who were in some cases tortured or raped. Perhaps surprisingly, these stories do not always deeply affect us. It depends very much on the way the respondent tells the story. Our consistent experience, in Kazakhstan, Malaysia, and Morocco, is that when respondents themselves appear to have processed what has happened to them, as a thing of the past, it is not shocking or traumatic for us to hear their experiences, even if they concern objectively painful events. When they tell us things they have already spoken about many times, rather than personally opening their hearts and sharing their pain or fear with us, the stories more readily take on the form of depersonalized data.

Conversely, a story does not need to be particularly gruesome to shock us, if it challenges our preconceptions of how things work, and the reality is more harsh. This was the experience of our Kazakhstan researcher when hearing what happened to her contact Irina, the director of an NGO she had long known. The NGO dealt with multiple issues, some of which are considered sensitive, and had previously had some bureaucratic difficulties, but always worked hard to maintain a relationship with the authorities. The evening before traveling to West Kazakhstan for an NGO event, Irina was attacked outside her apartment and robbed of her big purse full of documents, money for grants, hard disks, and everything necessary for the event. According to Irina and her colleagues, the attacker clearly must have known what was in the purse. A witness in a car refused to call the police; he was probably implicated. The event in West Kazakhstan then ran into other difficulties, with permits being revoked, and local hotels and the university refusing to host the event, compounding the likelihood that the attack was political in nature. Despite the fact that Irina was not physically hurt, our researcher was quite shocked by the story. She had previously been conscious that targeted violence was characteristic even of the 'soft authoritarian' context of Kazakhstan and had read of physical violence used by the regime before, but this was the first instance where it happened to someone she personally knew, which was like a revelation of something that had always been there but hidden in the background.

When we see our respondents in pain or afraid, especially when we come upon hard stories unexpectedly, the impact on us is much greater. This was the experience, for instance, of our Morocco researcher, who spent an afternoon meeting the members of an association for the rights of Salafist prisoners. She sat in a room full of women, the daughters, wives, and mothers of these prisoners. Each woman in turn told her story, and it was just one atrocity after the other. One ended her story about her son with 'and they condemned him to the death penalty'. Another appeared to have become mentally deranged as the result of the killing of her younger child and husband, and possible psychological torture. Had she been working for an organization like Amnesty International, our researcher might have been prepared to hear these stories, and would have known what to do with them: write a report. But she was unprepared, and felt alone against the ugliest part of humankind. During the meeting, our researcher remained clinical, asking questions, taking notes. She could not open the door to empathy because it would have overwhelmed her. The traumatic impact of these stories was compounded by the intrusive surveillance, described above, that followed immediately afterward, and by the pressure to get results, which we discuss further on in this chapter. For a time, she could not stop thinking about the stories, the derangement of one woman, the lifeless voice of another. Hiking, eating well, and spending time on her own eventually helped her recover.

Stories that unsettle us do not always come from those directly affected by them. Our Mexico researcher was shaken by the account of a forensic journalist who investigates crime scenes, including political murders. She told a story of careful planning and tremendous professionalism in the implementation of deliberately gruesome murders, intended to send a message to others. He was told similar stories by other respondents as well. Just like our Morocco researcher, his initial response was to get on with his work, ask more questions, analyze the situation, without considering the horror of what he had been told, and how it affected him personally. In fact, it is difficult to start processing the mental impact while in the field, when there are too many other things going on. We oftentimes need the safety of home, and the distance in time and space, to evaluate and deal with the impact the field has on us. If coping in the field becomes too hard, then going home early should be the obvious solution. However, as we will discuss below, the pressure to get results, and the shame of an unsuccessful trip can get in the way of such a sensible course of action.

The Field Stays with Us

One might assume that, since we are field researchers, bad incidents or stories that emotionally affect us are things that we should be prepared for during fieldwork, and then we go home and relax. We know political life in the 'field' does not stop when we take our plane, and we typically stay in touch, but still, the physical distance typically also translates into some emotional distance. But not always.

One of the more upsetting experiences our China researcher has had to deal with, happened in the United Kingdom. She acted as translator for a group of visiting Chinese local government officials from a region whose main city is famous for its peacefulness, quality of life, and international flavor, a reputation she had found confirmed during fieldwork. In her private conversation with one of the officials, she asked about a group of villagers who had occupied the highway in that locality, in a land-related protest. The protest had attracted a lot of attention, but then suddenly, all went quiet. She asked the local official what happened to the villagers, and he made an emphatic face and said: 'we dealt with it'. She asked, 'what do you mean?', but she knew very well what he meant. Our researcher was in no personal danger whatsoever in this exchange and had not even known the villagers. Nonetheless, she was shocked and saddened to hear directly from an individual who had chillingly 'dealt with' the villagers' rightful protest, even in this reputedly harmonious place.

Much more personal was the experience of our Mexico researcher. One of his main contacts during fieldwork had been a young photographer, Ruben Espinosa. Espinosa gave him several other contacts and sometimes came along to these other interviews too. Our researcher had interviewed him several times and also met him socially. He had been aware from the very first meeting that Ruben Espinosa had been threatened and feared being killed. A few months after the fieldwork, while he was at a conference, our researcher got a text message from another contact, telling him that Espinosa had been killed. It transpired that he had fled from the province of Veracruz to Mexico City, where he and four flatmates had been tortured and murdered. While nothing has been proven, it is widely assumed that this was a political murder, connected to an unflattering photograph and article about the provincial governor (Watson 2015;

Goldman 2015). Less than a year later, a second contact went missing and was later found shot. This was not a respondent, but an acquaintance from an earlier trip, from whose parents our researcher had rented an apartment during fieldwork. The circumstances of his death are less clear, but it was a violent death, and the motive may also have been political. Initially, our researcher responded by having intensive contact with Mexican friends, and by writing two online articles for a broader audience (Bartman 2015a, 2015b). This helped him feel that he was doing something to draw attention to the murder of journalists in Mexico. But it was not enough: he experienced trauma symptoms such as stress and insomnia and eventually sought counseling. This has taught him to approach traumatic events not just analytically, but to acknowledge the emotional impact: feelings of fear, anger, and guilt. He has also de-intensified his contact with people in the field, and does not contemplate going back to the same province in the near future. For the sake of optimal data-gathering, a repeat visit might have been desirable, but just as in the case of the research on Salafists in Morocco, it was deemed simply too risky to do so, even apart from the emotional strain.

Attending to and Coping with Mental Impact

The lesson from the experience described above is certainly not that everyone needs to seek counseling after authoritarian fieldwork, let alone before it. We should tread lightly, and not overburden first-time researchers with unnecessary expectations of getting traumatized. Most of us are not traumatized by the authoritarian field most of the time. Nonetheless, individually as well as collectively as an academic community, we should recognize that our fieldwork experiences can sometimes have a severe, perhaps even traumatic, emotional impact on us (see Loyle and Simoni 2017 for a more extensive plea for engagement with the possibility of trauma). This has not traditionally been a subject of academic attention, and the difficulty can be compounded by our sense that, compared to the suffering of some of our respondents, our own vicarious feelings are not worth mentioning. But we should attend to them, and we do not do our respondents a disservice by doing so.

NGO workers, whether they do human rights or humanitarian work, are trained in stress release and listening techniques, and typically debriefed after a stay in the field. We often go to the same places, and we also do difficult work. If stress release methods or debriefing works for them, we should at least consider as researchers whether it can help us too. How exactly we need to respond will be different for each person and each situation. For some, professional counseling is in order, for others, spiritual (self-)help is the best answer. At a minimum, we should talk to friends and colleagues about what has happened and its impact on us. Others too have found that 'maintaining meaningful contact with others (friends, family, professional networks) is one of the best ways to mitigate the potential impacts of trauma' (Loyle and Simoni 2017, referencing Dickson-Swift et al. 2008). We would argue that this is all the more important in authoritarian contexts, which are already liable to propel us in the direction of paranoia and mental isolation. This is borne out, for instance, by the experience of Begley, who investigated what was behind the apparent popular support for the RPF in Rwanda, and not only encountered constant surveillance but also had to worry, more than we have had to do, about the risk her interviews posed to respondents. She writes how '(t)hese fears added to the increasing feelings of frustration, constant mistrust, feelings of always being watched, and having no one who understood the situation to offer advice or support, essentially imprisoned me, leaving no secure way to communicate anything to anyone' (Begley 2013, 82; see also Malekzadeh 2016, 868). It appears to have been this sense of isolation as much as the fear itself that caused her to suffer from post-traumatic stress after fieldwork.

Apart from recognizing stress symptoms, and finding our own personal ways of addressing them, we should also consider how stressful incidents, hard stories or traumatic events affect our written work. We should reflect on the possible validity gain, but also the risk of bias or self-censorship, once we ourselves or people we know personally have suffered from forms of repression. The quality of our conversations with colleagues who rely on desk-based work stands to gain from such self-reflection. And we should reconsider, after stressful incidents, hard stories or traumatic events on what fields we are prepared to revisit; what topics we are, and are not, willing to explore; and what methods we want to employ, in future research.

Then there is physical impact. While our team had extensively prepared for the specificities of authoritarian fieldwork, and given some attention to potential mental impact, we had neglected to consider the combined physical impact of pollution, temperature changes, change of diet, and hard work. If we experience stressful incidents, hard stories or traumatic events as described above, our bodies take yet another hit from the psychosomatic effect of such occurrences. All but one of our team got sick during recent fieldwork trips, though some of us much worse than others. So here we have some very practical advice: do not go on fieldwork unless you are in top shape, and plan not just for political but also for medical emergencies, determine who you would turn to with simple or complex medical problems, and how you would go about getting home early if necessary. Lastly, we will consider mental impact in relation to another source of stress, which we discuss in our next section "Pressure to Get Results".

Pressure to Get Results

A subject that has had some attention, but not necessarily specifically in the context of authoritarian fieldwork, is the pressure, especially on early-career scholars, to get results and publish them. Unfortunately, this problem has primarily been framed in relation to the temptation to cut corners or commit scientific fraud. We have no knowledge, or even suspicions, of scholars of authoritarianism who responded to pressure to publish by simply making up results. But almost all of us have experienced mental stress at the thought of a failed fieldwork trip, coming home with insufficiently robust findings to publish as an article. We also know instances, in our own experience and that of others, where pressure to get results led to flawed decision-making in relation to risk. A final concern is scientific: not the temptation to invent empirical data but a tendency to prejudge conclusions, and to confirm our initial hunches rather than listen carefully and with openness to what the field is actually telling us.

The pressure to get results comes from three interrelated sources: from ourselves, through informal peer pressure from our colleagues, and from our institutional environments. Social scientists are typically self-starters; ours is a highly individualist profession that does not suit those who need constant external guidance and prodding to get to work. We are often our own hardest taskmasters. Especially during fieldwork periods, which are expensive in time and money, and hence precious, we are likely to feel particular pressure to get results. This may just make us a little overenthusiastic and reckless, which is how our Malaysia researcher interprets his brush with Malaysian plainclothes police, described in Chap. 2, with hindsight. But it may also turn into more fundamental self-doubt about what we are doing in the field, and what could be the consequences of 'no data'. Sæther, who did research on critical journalism in China, is a rare voice actually admitting—after the fact—that during her PhD fieldwork, there were '(d)ays wasted watching American DVDs, reading spy novels or in other profitless ways' and that these 'empty days made me doubt the entire project' and imagine 'that my stay would end up as a complete failure'. As she explains, these empty days are generally omitted from any description of fieldwork, 'which emphasizes the active approach taken by the field-worker' (Sæther (2006), 54–55, 43).

The sense of self-doubt may be exacerbated in contacts with colleagues. In our experience, discussing failure and frustration in field research is largely taboo. When you meet other researchers in the field, they may show off a little about their contacts and all the information they have gathered. Nobody will say 'I don't get interviews at all, things are going badly'. At conferences too, the assumption is always that you have results to share, they are not safe spaces to discuss difficulty in getting results. And yet, for many reasons detailed in the previous chapters, to do with prioritizing our own safety, with shifting red lines, or with reluctant respondents, authoritarian field research can simply fail. At least one of us, our Iran researcher, has experienced a field trip that yielded negligible results: at that time, about that topic, respondents simply would not talk to him. Our Kazakhstan researcher has not had such a disappointing experience in Kazakhstan itself, but hit a brick wall when trying to approach Kazakhstani students, and study their organizations, in the United Kingdom. Less dramatically, managing fewer interviews than you had wanted or expected is actually a pretty common experience.

The most consequential pressure to get results is hierarchical and institutional. PhD researchers, research assistants, and post-docs may experience pressure from their supervisor or project leader. They are expected to come back from the field with results. In our project, the project leader has in some cases put on the table in advance the possibility that, despite trying their very best, a researcher might come back more or less empty-handed because the 'field does not yield', but we do not think this is common practice. We believe that senior researchers in this field have a responsibility to create an environment in which the possibility of disappointing fieldwork can be openly discussed. But beyond a supervisor, there are the economic bottom lines of the broader institutional environment: job security and research funding simply depend on past results. At the time of writing, only one of us eight coauthors has a tenured position. For the others, failing fieldwork can have direct consequences on the job market.

It is this brute material fact that explains why our Morocco researcher went back for a second attempt at doing research on Salafists despite having been both traumatized by the stories of victims' relatives and intimidated by the security forces. She needed money to live and finish her PhD, as well as wanting to maintain professional relations with the senior researcher who led the project. After months of trying and failing, she finally gave up on the project. Today, with much more experience, a doctoral title and a lengthening string of publications, she feels she has more room for manoeuvre in selecting which topics to work on. A Russia researcher one of us heard speaking at a conference undertook an even greater risk to continue his research on ethno-religious profiling in the Northern Caucasus, in order to 'come back from my fieldwork and not be "ashamed" of my research results' (Ratelle 2013, 208). Taking advantage of his own muscular appearance and adding some details (growing a beard, carrying a backpack), he would go through security checkpoints and allow himself to be detained and sometimes roughed up, to be able to write about it. In this case, apart from some degree of bravado, the perceived need to 'come home with data' appears to have been what drove this young researcher, who now acknowledges suffering from post-traumatic stress disorder. These experiences chime with Loyle and Simoni's argument that graduate students and pretenure staff 'constitute a high-risk group when considering the impact of research-related trauma' (2017, 142), precisely because the impact of exposure to violence and suffering is compounded by the pressure to get results. We cannot, and probably do not want to, fundamentally challenge an academic system that rewards theory-building based on solid data. But we do have a responsibility as an academic community to teach young researchers that no data-gathering for the sake of a career is worth knowingly putting ourselves through extreme treatment.

Positive Mental Impact

Contrary to what this chapter may have appeared to suggest so far, the mental impact of authoritarian field research does not just come in the form of frustration, fear, trauma, or stress. It has positive impacts too. Malekzadeh describes authoritarian field research as restorative, by which he means 'restorative of "the local" even as it informs nonlocal audiences outside of the case' (2016, 873, see also 862). We agree, but also find it restorative in another sense: inspiring and uplifting. We find that speaking to many different kinds of people in the authoritarian field has made us question some of our prior assumptions and ideas. It has helped us come to the full realization that what we do is *social* science: the stuff we study is about human beings, with all their complexities. Conducting many interviews has also helped us to be good listeners, which we find valuable not just as researchers, but as people. Fieldwork, in sum, has made us more open-minded, humble, and thoughtful.

Chapter Conclusion: Talk About It

In this chapter, we have discussed a number of issues that are rarely discussed in authoritarianism research: physical impact, surveillance, fear, betrayal, hard stories, traumatization, and pressure to get results. We want to stress that some of the events we have described are relatively rare. Authoritarianism research is mostly uneventful, and not particularly gruesome. But bad things do happen, to us and our respondents, and there are no easy fixes for either avoiding or dealing with them. Our best advice is to do precisely what we have done in these pages: talk about it, before, during, and after fieldwork.

During fieldwork, it is important to invest in 'warm contacts'. This is valuable not only because of the introductions they can make for us, or their analytical help, but also for our own well-being. We already discussed in Chap. 4 that trust is both a very valuable and a fragile commodity in authoritarian contexts. For our own sakes too, without trusting people unconditionally or unnecessarily sharing sensitive information with them, it can be useful to confide our insecurities and hesitations with a few people with whom we feel an easy connection. Some of us have experienced that when we isolate ourselves, we start overthinking our situation and getting negative thoughts. Our Iranian researcher believes that he would have understood the position of his rogue friend better and earlier if he had been more willing to discuss the situation with Iranian friends. Our China researcher found that it helped to share her sadness over the chilling fate of the protesting villagers with her supervisor. Our Malaysia researcher recovered his confidence after the incident with plainclothes policemen by talking to locals about it. Our Kazakhstan researcher found her severe and mysterious health problems in the field easier to bear because she was looked after by a friend.

During and after fieldwork, it is also useful to talk to colleagues about our frustrations and doubts about our work. When our research results are suboptimal, we are easily inclined to think we did something wrong: that we were too naïve, too reckless, or conversely we were too cautious and too self-censoring, and we could have had better results if we had acted differently. Our academic culture is not such that we readily talk about problems in field research. But having tried it, we have found it really useful to share experiences. It makes us feel better, sometimes do our research better, and sometimes learn that we could probably not have done it better.

References

Barros, R. (2016). On the Outside Looking In: Secrecy and the Study of Authoritarian Regimes. *Social Science Quarterly, 97*, 964–965. https://doi.org/10.1111/ssqu.12350.

Bartman, J. (2015a). Wederom Journalist Vermoord in Mexico. *Stuk Rood Vlees, 8*. Retrieved from http://stukroodvlees.nl/wederom-journalist-vermoord-in-mexico/.

Bartman, J. (2015b). Mexico's Deadly Truths. *OpenDemocracy, 25*. Retrieved from https://www.opendemocracy.net/jos-bartman/mexico%E2%80%99s-deadly-truths.

Begley, L. (2013). The RPF Control Everything! Fear and Rumour under Rwanda's Genocide Ideology Legislation. In S. Thomson, A. Ansoms, & J. Murison (Eds.), *Emotional and Ethical Challenges for Field Research in Africa: The Story Behind the Findings* (pp. 70–84). London: Palgrave Macmillan.

Goldman, F. (2015). Who Killed Rubén Espinosa and Nadia Vera. *New Yorker Magazine*. Retrieved July 14, 2017, from http://www.newyorker.com/news/news-desk/who-killed-ruben-espinosa-and-nadia-vera.

Loyle, C., & Simoni, A. (2017). Researching Under Fire: Political Science and Researcher Trauma. *PS: Political Science & Politics, 50*, 141–145. https://doi.org/10.1017/S1049096516002328.

Malekzadeh, S. (2016). Paranoia and Perspective, or How I Learned to Stop Worrying and Start Loving Research in the Islamic Republic of Iran. *Social Science Quarterly, 97*, 862–875. https://doi.org/10.1111/ssqu.12342.

Privacy International. (2015). Stories of Surveillances in Morocco. Retrieved July 15, 2017, from https://www.privacyinternational.org/node/551.

Ratelle, J. (2013). *Radical Islam and the Chechen War Spillover: A Political Ethnographic Reassessment of the Upsurge of Violence in the North Caucasus Since 2009*. Ph.D., University of Ottawa. Retrieved from https://ruor.uottawa.ca/bitstream/10393/23791/1/Ratelle_Jean-Fran%C3%A7ois_2013_thesis.pdf.

Sæther, E. (2006). Fieldwork as Coping and Learning. In M. Heimer & S. Thøgersen (Eds.), *Doing Fieldwork in China* (pp. 42–58). Copenhagen: NIAS Press.

Watson, K. (2015). Impunity Feared in Mexico Photojournalist's Murder. *BBC*, 10 August. Retrieved July 14, 2017, from http://www.bbc.com/news/world-latin-america-33846438.

CHAPTER 6

Writing It Up

Abstract In this chapter, we reflect on standards relating to writing up and publishing research based on authoritarian fieldwork. After briefly relating the history of recent transparency initiatives, we first report extensively on our own current practices in relation to anonymization, protection, and transparency. Then, we make some recommendations regarding how the tension between the value of anonymity and the value of transparency might be better navigated, if not resolved. We make two proposals: the first concerns a shift from transparency about the identity of our sources to transparency about our methods of working. The second is to promote a culture of controlled sharing of anonymized sources. Finally, we reflect on trade-offs between publicly criticizing authoritarian regimes and future access to the authoritarian field.

Keywords Authoritarianism • Field research • Publishing • Transparency • Anonymity • Dissemination

In this chapter, we reflect, and make recommendations, on standards relating to writing up and publishing research based on authoritarian fieldwork. We do so at a time when many scientists in all disciplines are finding their role in society becoming less self-evident, and some feel that new measures are necessary to buttress the credibility and legitimacy of science. Such measures are intended to make our work more transparent,

M. Glasius et al., *Research, Ethics and Risk in the Authoritarian Field*,
https://doi.org/10.1007/978-3-319-68966-1_6

but they raise many questions and challenges, particularly but by no means exclusively for scholars in the authoritarian field. After briefly relating the history of recent transparency initiatives, which may not be familiar to all readers, we first report extensively on our own current practices in relation to anonymization, protection, and transparency. Subsequently, we make some recommendations regarding how the tension between the value of anonymity and the value of transparency might be better navigated, if not resolved. We make two proposals: the first concerns a shift from transparency about the identity of our sources to transparency about our methods of working. The second is to promote a culture of controlled sharing of anonymized sources. Finally, we reflect on trade-offs between publicly criticizing authoritarian regimes and future access to the authoritarian field.

The Call for Transparency

In 2017, scientists in 600 cities undertook the first ever March for Science, believing that scientific 'values are currently at risk', and that '(w)hen science is threatened, so is the society that scientists uphold and protect' (Principles and Goals, March for Science 2017). Actually, it is not clear that there is a general decline of trust in science (see, for instance, Pew Center 2017). Nonetheless, social scientists, like others, have felt under increased pressure to explain and justify why they deserve public funding and how their methods hold up to scrutiny. In political science, one response to this has been a change in the Ethics Guide of the American Political Science Association in 2012, reflecting the so-called Data Access and Research Transparency (DA-RT) principles. Subsequently, a number of leading political science journals have adopted a Journal Editors' Transparency Statement (JETS) (https://www.dartstatement.org), which constitutes an operationalization of the DA-RT principles form the perspective of journal editors. DA-RT states that 'researchers should provide access to … data or explain why they cannot', and JETS operationalizes this by committing journal editors to '(r)equire authors to ensure that cited data are available at the time of publication through a trusted digital repository'. While journal editors would be at liberty to grant exemptions, the new standard intended by JETS is full publication of raw data.

From late 2014, these statements became subject to increasing controversy, and a petition signed by many leading political scientists requested a delay in the implementation of DA-RT and more specifically JETS. The ethical and epistemological implications of these statements for various types of qualitative research, they argued, had not been sufficiently thought through. A lively debate on the implications of DA-RT has since ensued especially among primarily US-based political scientists (see https://dialogueondart.org and https://www.qualtd.net).

Whereas US debates on transparency have been motivated by concerns about scientific legitimacy and reliability probes, recent European initiatives promoting 'open science' have been more government-driven, arguing that data-sharing accelerates innovation, and could give Europe a competitive edge. In practical terms, they have focused on developing institutional digital storing and archiving capabilities rather than on changing editorial practices of journals (Directorate-General, Research & Innovation 2016). In a recent position paper, Germany and the Netherlands proposed the fast-track development of a 'European Open Science Cloud' (EOSC), which is to be 'a trusted, open environment for European researchers for the handling of all phases of the data life cycle and generated results'. The principle underlying the cloud is 'to make research data findable, accessible, interoperable and re-usable (FAIR)' (Joint Position Paper 2017, 1). What these European policy plans have in common with the US initiatives is the sense of urgency and universal applicability with which its proponents contend that all data should become open to all, as soon as possible.

Some scholars have already published their reflections, particularly in response to DA-RT, on tensions between transparency obligations and protection of respondents in specific authoritarian contexts (Driscoll 2015; Shih 2015; Lynch 2016). However, these comments tend to focus more on why DA-RT and JETS are problematic than on what *should* be considered best practice. And unlike DA-RT and JETS, the European 'open science' initiatives have yet to generate extensive debate within the political science profession. Hence, we find more extensive reflection, and making recommendations, on standards relating to writing up and publishing research-based authoritarian fieldwork desirable.

While, as we have reflected in previous chapters, the sources we collect in the field are much broader than interviews, we will focus the discussion on interview practices, because this is the area where the tension between transparency and the 'do no harm' imperative is most evident. When we conduct interviews, we always begin with a little opening speech explaining who we are and what kind of research we are doing and explaining that we will transcribe the interview, the transcript stays with us, but we may quote from it in academic publications. We always deal with the matter of informed consent orally. None of us has ever used informed consent forms. To our knowledge, they are not customary in authoritarianism research. They can cause distrust among respondents ('why do I need to sign something?'), as well as bringing about a potentially risky paper trail during fieldwork. At this point, our practices diverge, depending on the type of respondent. We discern roughly three categories of respondents. The first type, 'ordinary people', we typically inform that we intend to anonymize the transcript of the interview and not use their real name if we should cite them. With the second type, 'expert informants', we typically have an exchange about whether and if so how they would like to be anonymized. The third type are 'spokespersons', whom we typically ask for their permission to be cited by name.

Interviews with 'Ordinary People'

The default option of anonymity we find most appropriate when we interview certain categories of 'ordinary people'. Thus, our Kazakhstan researcher has used this when interviewing young Kazakhs who had studied or were studying abroad. Our Malaysia researcher used it when interviewing people about their decision-making as to whether to join a demonstration. We find the default option of anonymity appropriate in these cases for three reasons. First, as 'ordinary citizens', these people have typically not chosen to be professionally engaged with politics, they are usually not accustomed to being interviewed and cited, and they thus deserve a high level of protection of their privacy. Secondly, while some respondents might simply refuse to speak to us if we were to cite them by name, others might well agree to be interviewed, but we believe that the validity of their answers to our questions might suffer if they knew they could be quoted by name. This is an issue that is not unique to authoritarianism research, it would apply to interviews with vulnerable groups (i.e. victims of sexual abuse, undocumented migrants, or drug users) in democratic societies as well. In an authoritarian context, all ordinary citizens are in the 'vulnerable' category when we ask them questions that relate to their views of their government or dissident behavior. This is not to suggest that they would be in immediate fear of arrest or worse. In both cases we mentioned here, Kazakhstani students and Malaysian potential demonstrators, respondent concerns related more to their professional environment, their relation to their university, or even their family, all of which might disapprove of dissident views or behavior. Finally, we think anonymity is not problematic in this particular category because the respondents do not have access to unique information as individuals. These kinds of interviews are more akin to surveys in that sense. What makes them different from surveys is that we do not claim that the people we speak to are representative for a broader group, and we do not attempt to quantify their opinions or experiences. Instead of reliability, it is validity we are after, trying to reconstruct and reflect their thought processes in relation to at least somewhat politically sensitive issues. In these instances, our sampling method may be questioned, but not the anonymity as such.

Interviews with 'Expert Informants'

Most of the interviews we conduct in authoritarian settings fall into a different category, one that leads us to give respondents a choice when it comes to anonymity. We find this appropriate when interviewing lower-level government or party officials, corporate executives, journalists, local academics, opposition politicians, and activists. The reason we want to interview these people is usually that they can give us some insight into how the authoritarian system works in practice: within the bureaucracy or the party, in its dealings with other politically relevant actors, or in its dealings with critics. Revealing such information can make them vulnerable, although this does not always need to be the case. By anonymizing them (in such a way that they are genuinely unrecognizable, see below) we exclude any such risk. But it requires us to relax the ideal of complete transparency in how we come by our findings. If we cannot tell readers who we spoke to, they cannot trace whether we quoted and interpreted these sources accurately. We will reflect on this trade-off in more detail below.

Our experiences with the degree to which this second, broad category of respondents take us up on our offer of anonymity is very varied, depending on the repressiveness of the regime, the type of respondents, and the nature of our research question. Our Malaysia researcher found that the activists he interviewed were all but one entirely comfortable with being named. Their status as dissidents and members of a social movement in opposition to the government was well known, and while the answers to questions asked by our researcher were more specific than what they have publicly said online, they were not more incendiary. Our China researcher by contrast finds that both public officials and corporate employees almost always prefer anonymity. She still asks them, but she already knows what the answer will be. Most of us have experienced getting mixed responses in this category. When we have a mixed response, we have a difficult choice. It is clear that we cannot name respondents who have asked to be anonymized, but should we always name the ones who have told us they are comfortable with doing so? From the perspective of transparency, this would be the best option, but we find that there may be three reasons to act otherwise.

The first is homogeneity. In her research on municipal governance, for instance, our Morocco researcher felt that it did not make sense to anonymize a civil servant for one municipality, but not someone in the same position for another municipality. Likewise, our China and Iran researchers, who both interviewed people working for Internet companies who deal with government agencies, did not believe there was value added in providing some of their names but not others. Others in our group however believe that stylistic homogeneity should not be a priority, and every respondent who can be named represents a transparency gain and should therefore be named.

A second consideration is whether we sometimes feel that what we are being told is quite sensitive, and whether perhaps the respondent requires more protection than he or she is asking from us. This was a choice consistently made by Driscoll (2015), who interviewed Tajik or Afghan former militia members in an authoritarian but also volatile environment. He writes that '(i)n a few cases, the subject insisted that I record his full name. For my own safety, and that of my respondents, I never complied with these requests'. If we make such a judgment, we are in effect second-guessing our respondent's own judgment, as well as foregoing transparency. Nonetheless, some of us have occasionally made such a judgment. In the municipal research quoted above, our Morocco researcher came across a respondent who gave her highly sensitive information, really explaining how the administrative system exerted power over elected officials. He did not think he required anonymity, but she believed this was perhaps a little naïve, and he was saying things that would undoubtedly make his boss unhappy, and his boss's boss, all the way up to the top. So she decided that it was better to be overprotective than sorry and anonymized his statements. Our Mexico researcher has anonymized all journalist-respondents in a journal article, whether they had asked him to or not, but has yet to decide what to do in his dissertation. On the one hand, as discussed in Chap. 5, the context is very repressive, with murder a regular outcome for critical journalists. On the other hand, the journalists in question are already openly critical of the government and do not reveal much to our researcher that they have not said or written before, so the additional risk flowing from his published work may be quite limited. In fact, some activists actually seek—preferably international—visibility, not only to advertise their cause but also because they believe it gives them some level of protection. When a respondent articulates such a strategy, it would not make sense to overrule him or her for their protection.

A final reason to anonymize a respondent without being asked to do so can be the long delays in the publishing process, and a change in the situation on the ground during this process. Information that was not sensitive when provided may become sensitive by the time it is published. One of us, for instance, had the consent of (some) Egyptian activists to be mentioned by their first name in early 2013, but decided because of the subsequent military crackdown, that in subsequent publications they needed to be given aliases for their protection.

Interviews with 'Spokespersons'

The third category of interviews is where we speak to high-profile politicians or civil society figures on their official stance, as our China, Kazakhstan, and Morocco researchers have all done on occasion. We may still put anonymity on the table as an option, especially if we do not know in advance exactly how the interview is going to go, but we do not usually expect them to take it up. These are public figures who are used to media exposure (albeit in the constrained circumstances of their authoritarian context), and in some cases, they may have already spoken of the same topics on public occasions. They will know exactly what they want to say to us, and how to say it. Moreover, their quotes are only meaningful in the context of who they are. What they say to us is interesting not because they give us insight into their thought process, or into the inner workings of the bureaucracy or the political process, but because they are the head of the Islamist Party or the president of the biggest women's rights association. These kinds of interviewees will often give their consent to be quoted by name in our published work as a matter of course, although they may also give us some off-the-record information at the same time. Even if they only give us their official views, this can be of interest, because they give us insight into authoritarian legitimation strategies. But they typically only give us one face of authoritarian political processes: the public face. For some of our research, that is all we need, but for many other research questions, it is not enough.

Protective Practices

Not mentioning a name in our published work is only a small part of our anonymization practices. When we do not use real names, we use different kinds of descriptors instead. When respondents have very similar profiles, sometimes we just number them. Our Mexico researcher, for instance, just refers to journalist 1, journalist 2, and so on. Sometimes, especially when it comes to 'ordinary people' interviews such as those done by our Kazakhstan and our Malaysia researcher, we give our respondents aliases, fake first names. This improves readability and makes it possible for a reader to track particular respondents in a publication. When we have interviewed people in the second category, we try to convey some additional information, so that the reader can understand why the respondent in question would have a uniquely relevant perspective on the matter at hand, while still not making them traceable. We might refer to them as 'senior manager at Baidu, Beijing', or 'journalist, target of phishing attempts'. Sometimes, we need to omit more than a name to keep someone's identity a secret (see Shih 2015, 22 for some very concrete examples on how to be protective while still conveying to a reader why a respondent could be considered as a well-informed source). A Malaysian civil servant who had attended an anti-government demonstration, for instance, insisted that it was not enough to delete his name; any detailed information concerning his workplace could make him traceable, so the researcher used the vague reference 'works for the government'.

But anonymization is not just about what eventually gets published. When a respondent asks to remain anonymous, we always keep their real names separate from our transcript. The real names may be found in our notes, in an old diary, or in a document kept separate from the transcripts. Contact details are also kept separate from transcripts (see also Shih 2015, 22). We are well aware that none of these practices is completely secure. While we are in the field, we are in possession both of a set of contact details with identifiers (real names or not) and a set of transcripts. If someone were to steal or forcibly seize all our notes, transcripts, and recordings (which is in some contexts much more likely than high-tech electronic surveillance, as graphically depicted in Driscoll 2015, 6), and study them attentively, they would probably be able to trace the respondents. In some cases, the transcripts themselves are actually revealing, as, for instance, in the case of our Mexico researcher, whose journalist-respondents sometimes refer to their own published work. At other times, it would be a matter of putting together the transcripts and our other information. None of us have been in a position where our material was taken from us during fieldwork (although a bag containing fieldwork material was once stolen during transit, see Chap.2), but it *can* happen. Our protective practices would make it time-consuming and difficult to trace respondents, but we cannot guarantee that it would be impossible.

As Bellin (2016) has pointed out, such risks put us under an ethical obligation to be transparent in quite a different way from that intended by DA-RT or 'open science': transparency to our research subjects (see also Loyle 2016), resulting in 'a negotiation of the level of risk and disclosure that the respondents are comfortable with' (https://www.qualtd.net, IV.1). While we endorse the spirit of this, we do not think that her proposal that in the writing-up phase 'the respondents work with the researcher to specify what identifying information can be written about and what should be removed or altered' is always practicable. Precisely when working with respondents who may be at risk, we cannot assume that our—usually digital—communications with them about such matters would be safe. We may sometimes have to take decisions about altered risk conditions for them, as in the case of Egyptian activists referred to above.

Off-the-Record Information

We also come across information in our research that we cannot use at all, not even on condition of anonymity. Sometimes, such information is really of no interest to us, so we just ignore it. Our Malaysia researcher, for instance, found that his activist respondents would sometimes disparage each other off the record, but their internal relations had little to do with his research question. It becomes more difficult when they do give us information that is important, and is either new, or corroborates other evidence. Our India researcher has literally had the experience of a respondent who had given permission for a recorded interview changing his mind and asking for the recording to be erased. When such a request is made, whether we think it is reasonable or not, no visible trace of the information should remain in our published work. But what cannot be asked of us is that we erase the information from our minds. If it is indeed important, it will inform our analysis, and we may look for other sources for the same information. In this case, other interviews confirmed the story the respondent had told. Our Kazakhstan researcher has likewise had relevant information from an opposition source who emphatically asked that what he said be kept confidential, since the information 'would put him in a situation of risk'. She tried to find written sources to corroborate the factual information he had given and kept the opinions he had expressed in the back of her mind during her analysis. In both of these cases, the off-the-record information was of some use to the researchers, but in both cases, it resulted in the written analysis looking less solid than it actually was, because it rested on an additional source that could not be mentioned at all.

Anonymity vs. Transparency

The primary reason not to insist on divulging sources has already been mentioned and is widely acknowledged as taking precedence over the merits of research transparency: respondents in precarious circumstances require our protection (Ahram and Goode 2016; Bellin 2016; Driscoll 2015; Lynch 2016; Shih 2015; Stroschein 2016). The value of anonymity is not unique to authoritarianism research, or even to research on vulnerable groups in the social sciences. It also applies to medical research, or public opinion research. In this sense, transparency is never boundless in academia. As we have argued above, we think anonymity is relatively unproblematic when it comes to research on random members of a subgroup of the general population. Anonymity becomes more controversial when we rely on respondents who have specific, privileged knowledge of the workings of the authoritarian system and who are not interchangeable with others. Using what these kinds of respondents tell us under condition of anonymity poses a dilemma between transparency and anonymity. Betraying their confidence goes against the do-no-harm principle and is ethically unconscionable. So the only other alternative would be not to publish anything that would have to rely on anonymous sources, which raises its own ethical challenges, since it furthers the interests of authoritarian powerholders in opaqueness and potentially ignores voices that can and want to tell us about abusive practices. It is possible in principle to do authoritarianism research entirely based on named sources, for instance, by focusing on historic cases (Art 2016). But we believe that in our field of research—as well as many others—too much would get lost. Each of us, in many different contexts, has at times relied on anonymity. In our experience, those of our 'authoritarianism' colleagues who rely on field research as a primary source have almost all done so too. We believe that it is fair to say that the field could not exist without it.

Transparency About Our Practices, Not Our Respondents

None of us think reliance on anonymous sources is unproblematic from a scientific point of view. Whether or not we believe in actual replicability of our kind of research (we are divided on this), we all think that transparency is required for other academics to judge our work, and to build on it. None of us have published work that rests entirely on anonymous sources. Indeed we agree with the advice given by Shih (2015) and Bellin (comment on https://www.qualtd.net, IV.1, 2016) that authoritarianism research should not fetishize the interview as the only or best source of information but triangulate information from interview material with public documents or online sources. Some of us even think work that relies entirely on anonymous sources should not be published because it is not even partially verifiable. Others think that under very specific circumstances, when the author can argue why there was no safe alternative way of gaining relevant insights, such publications can be permissible. But instead of arguing about precisely how much a publication should be allowed to rely on anonymous sources, we find it more helpful to shift the way we think about transparency from a primary focus on the identity of our sources to a focus on increasing transparency about our methods of working.

Publications that rely on qualitative research are wildly variable in the attention they give to research methods, depending on their disciplinary or subdisciplinary traditions and epistemological orientations. In some journals, the standard is for qualitative research to be written up in ways that approximate as closely as possible the manner in which quantitative research is conducted and described, which is not always appropriate and helpful. In other subdisciplines and associated journals, there is simply no tradition of requiring a methodology section giving attention to how the empirical material was gathered and analyzed. We think that there are many ways of doing good authoritarianism research, but regardless whether it aims to substantiate causal claims or whether it is more exploratory or interpretive in nature, it always benefits from transparency about how we do things. We would argue for more transparency than is currently customary in our field of research. The spotlight should be not on the identity of the sources but on the practices of the researcher. We already typically share when an interview took place (where it took place is occasionally sensitive, see Shih 2015, 22), so that at a minimum we could, when challenged, prove that we were 'in the field' on that day, rather than behind our desk inventing respondents, but that is just fraud-proofing. We can do more: share how we came by respondents, and what biases there might be in that process, give insight into the kinds of questions we asked, into the informed consent-related conversations we had with respondents, whether we recorded, how we treated our material, and so on. There should also always be a justification, which can be brief if it is relatively obvious, of why certain sources need to be kept anonymous. As Shih proposes, scholars of authoritarianism could also be more explicit about the other ways in which research has been tailored to meet constraints imposed by the regime, making it clear, for instance, that in undertaking a survey, we might 'ask proxy questions that are highly correlated with the sensitive questions' (Shih 2015, 20–21). Our choices regarding methods, ethics, and integrity could all be treated in one section, or if being transparent eats too much into our word count, they can be elaborated in an online appendix.

A Culture of Controlled Sharing

When it comes to sharing of sources, one might think that while the *identity* of our respondents often needs to be secret, the material itself could be shared with all, just as the raw data underlying medical research or population statistics can be made public. Why do we not just put anonymized transcripts online? While one of us has indeed done so in the past, we think that too often, doing so would still put our respondents at risk. Precisely because they are not random respondents, but people with specific expertise or privileged information, a good secret service can come to understand who you have been talking to, either from the transcripts alone, or by combining it with their other information about you, or your respondents (see also Tripp's comment on https://www.qualtd.net, IV.1, 2016). We also believe it unlikely that respondents who want to remain anonymous would readily give their consent to having the entire transcript of the interview made publicly available. And if they did, the information they would give us might be a lot less valuable: having a conversation with us, after carefully having built a relation of trust (see Chap. 4) is not the same as making a broadcast—even an anonymized broadcast—to the world. Transcripts cannot therefore be available to everybody.

A final reason for not making interview transcripts publicly available is that we believe anonymized transcripts would in fact be of limited value to other scholars. Transcripts are faithful transcriptions of a conversation, but they cannot be readily interpreted without the requisite contextual knowledge, the relation to off-the-record comments possibly made during the interview itself, the connection with other conversations that could not be transcribed, and so on. They are not equivalent to quantitative data, and our process of drawing conclusions from them cannot be replicated in the same way quantitative procedures can be replicated on the basis of the data and code by anyone with the requisite methodological skills.

Nonetheless, we think that the current practice of saying 'just trust us', and keeping transcripts entirely to ourselves, is not good for our collective reputation as academics. We believe a culture of qualified sharing of anonymized transcripts should be fostered in our field, and perhaps also in relation to qualitative research with vulnerable respondents more widely. We will describe two concrete ways in which we imagine that this can work, which should be read as complementary to each other.

The first is sharing between colleagues, usually but not necessarily within the same department. Within our project, we share all anonymized transcripts with each other. We do not share real names with each other: the only benefit of sharing real names we can think of would be to further reduce the likelihood of fraud, but as we discuss below, we do not think it plausible that researchers can and will invent reams of pages of false transcripts. What sharing means to us in practice is that transcripts are all stored together on an offline laptop in our office. It is a system to guarantee that a small number of people have seen the interviews and can confirm their existence. In case of a doctoral candidate struggling to turn his material into an argument, moreover, supervisors can actually review the material and offer better advice. This is an obvious and attractive solution for research groups such as ours. Such groups are increasingly prevalent in Europe due to the current nature of funding, which favors personal grants to mid-career or senior scholars, intended for building a group around a project. It may also work for region-based research centers, that is, centers for Middle Eastern studies and China or Russia studies, where there is an institutional awareness of the specificities of our work. We would be more hesitant to recommend it as a solution in all circumstances: in general political science departments, there may not be the same understanding of the sensitivity of the material, or conversely, the practice might lapse because nobody polices it. A drawback of sharing within a group or center is that, in case there are concerns over authenticity, close colleagues may have a personal or institutional stake in covering for each other. But this kind of sharing is still to be preferred over not sharing at all, which we believe to be the current standard, and it can be combined with other sharing practices as described below.

A second sharing practice could emerge in the context of the publication process of a journal article or book manuscript. One form this could take is peer review: either transcripts could be shared with reviewers as a matter of course, or there could be a designated 'source reviewer'. We think most authoritarianism researchers would be reluctant to accept such a system: given that most peer review is double-blind, it would require authors to hand over transcripts without having any idea to whom, other than that these people are presumably also academics. Researchers might well feel that submitting transcripts in this way would breach their obligation to their respondents. Moreover, it would place a heavy burden of responsibility on journal editors or book publishers, who would then be responsible not only for the academic quality of the reviewer but also for her integrity with regard to neither using the transcripts for their own purposes nor sharing them with third parties.

A more obvious solution, we think, is that anonymized transcripts can be shared with editors. As researchers, we know who the editors are, and we have chosen their particular journal or publishing house as our preferred outlet, so it would not be strange to be asked to share transcripts with them. Editors act as guarantors of quality, and this could extend to due diligence in terms of checking the authenticity of sources. The exact way in which this would work could be a matter of editorial policy. Given the burden on editors, we imagine they might not ask for and actually check through transcripts for every manuscript that relies on anonymized sources. They might check for a random sample, or ask for transcripts when they themselves or reviewers have concerns about authenticity, or both. We have to admit that sharing with editors is not absolute guarantee against fraud: unless recordings are shared, there is always a theoretical possibility that a researcher would invent entire transcripts. We think it implausible, however, that anyone who had the local knowledge *and* creative talent to do so would use their capabilities to diligently conjure up lengthy exchanges with non-existent respondents.

In our conception, only confidential materials explicitly referred to in publications should be subject to sharing. We concur with Lynch (2016, 38) and Tripp (https://www.qualtd.net, IV.1, 2016) that it makes little sense to share our multilingual fieldnote scribbles, which will not be intelligible to anyone. Nor should we be under an obligation to make them intelligible, any more than we should be obliged to reconstruct inspirational thoughts we may have in the shower before writing them up. We acknowledge that editors will not be in a position to fully interpret transcripts. As we explained above, seeing transcripts does not imply that you can 'replicate' the analysis. Finally, there are practical challenges, for which we do not yet have adequate solutions to offer, concerning how to securely transmit transcripts to an editor. But our position is that we should move toward a culture where it would be considered natural and legitimate for editors to ask to see anonymized transcripts that we refer to in publications, and we would share them on request. It cannot be the case that while quantitative researchers are increasingly being asked to make raw data publicly available, we will not share any of our material with anyone and just insist on being trusted.

Archiving Our Transcripts

As we explained in our introduction to this chapter, recent European policy initiatives aim to create a 'network of networks' of digital data repositories. It is still quite unclear at what point a researcher would be expected to place data in a digital repository, and to what extent access would indeed be open to all. The notion in a recent policy paper that all data should be available to all, in all phases of the research cycle (Joint Policy Paper 2017) reflects a poor understanding of how scientists work, and governmental overreach in terms of transforming their ways of working. Nonetheless, social science researchers in Europe may soon come under institutional pressure to comply with mandatory data storage in digital repositories. Open access repositories are subject to exactly the same objections as the DA-RT and JETS initiatives, specifically but not exclusively from the perspective of the authoritarian field, so we need not rehearse our arguments here.

But we want to go a step further and state our objections even to digital repositories with restricted and/or embargoed access. Again, our primary objection concerns risk to respondents. As Marc Lynch points out, 'the difficulty of guaranteeing confidentiality for materials deposited in a trusted repository are not hypothetical to those of us who conduct research in the Middle East and North Africa' (Lynch 2016, 37), and the same is true for other authoritarian contexts. We discern three aspects to this risk of breaching confidentiality, and hence risking harm: political contingency, legal risk, and digital risk. The first aspect relates to the apparently very reasonable suggestion that we could place our material in digital repositories under embargo, to be made public after, for instance, five or ten years, subject to our consent. The problem with this is that we cannot predict the future, and hence we cannot assume that publishing transcripts would gradually become less sensitive over time. It can also become more dangerous. Lynch gives the example of Egypt, already referred to above: what were 'bold but safe' statements made by activists in 2012 or the first half of 2013 quickly became very dangerous from the latter half of 2013. Stroschein gives the similar example of Turkey, which has become much more repressive after the coup attempt of 2016 (https://www.qualtd.net, IV.1). A disembargoed interview with a Turkish respondent from, say 2011, could well land her in trouble in 2017. And as we discussed in Chap. 3, our China researcher has seen a more subtle but discernible shift in the 'red lines' of permissibility in China over the past years, that could have implications for disembargoed transcripts.

Second, there is the possibility of transcripts becoming subject to legal subpoena, a particular concern with US scholars (Driscoll 2015, 6; Lynch 2016). We have not given attention in this book to the risk of legal subpoena, because we have no personal experience with it, and it still seems to be a rare occurrence. But what we can say is that when we store materials in a digital repository, we give up control: the (difficult) choice of weighing responsibility toward respondents against legal obligations and possible criminal liability would no longer be ours to make. Driscoll (2015, 6) records actually having burnt some of his field materials in order to guard against the risk of subpoena. None of us have gone this far, but we are aware that ethical review boards sometimes insist on the destruction of data to protect respondents. A blanket destruction requirement would be just as extreme as a blanket transparency requirement, but the fact that social scientists can be subject to both contradictory prescriptions at the same time illustrates the unhelpfulness of blunt, one-size-fits-all solutions to research dilemmas.

Finally, even if deposited transcripts were to remain in restricted access, it would be naïve, in the age of hacking, to believe that academic repositories can be made fully secure. We would like to believe that most secret services most of the time have other priorities than getting access to our transcripts, but we can never be certain. In Chap. 4, we quoted the forthright answer one of us got from a Moroccan activist when she asked him a sensitive question: 'if you can assure me that you can protect me I will give you my answer … but since you cannot, I will not'. Here, we paraphrase him to state our position on storing sensitive interview transcripts in digital repositories: if the institution can assure us that it can protect our respondents, we will give it our transcripts, but since it cannot, we will not.

Writing, Dissemination, and Future Access

As academics, we all want our work to be paid attention, by our peers but perhaps also beyond academia. We may even dream of being famous as academics. But for a researcher on authoritarianism, academic fame is a double-edged sword. If more than a handful of colleagues are taking notice of our work, the regime may be doing so too. As we described in earlier chapters of this book, we all do research in contexts where there is some degree of space for, and understanding of, social science research. But this space is constrained, and we do carefully consider what we publish, where we publish, and how we disseminate our work.

Our Kazakhstan researcher suspects that the regime would not be happy about some of her work, especially that which focuses on the workings of the party in power. She did consider this when writing, but she believes that most political leaders will not read it, and even if they should read it, they would still assume that, as an academic paper, it would be mostly ignored or considered harmless because it does not communicate directly with a large public. She faced a dilemma when an assistant to the prime minister specifically asked to be sent a copy of her work on the political leadership's legitimation strategies (Del Sordi 2016). Since the assistant had been very helpful and had agreed to be interviewed herself, our researcher could not refuse, but she did have some concern that her access to the country could be jeopardized by this move. The prime minister in question has a reputation for academic curiosity, however, and she has not in fact had difficulties with her most recent visa. She has even seen colleagues taking a more public critical position without consequences for their access, but as the authorities are always weighing the reputational consequences of denying access against those of being criticized, one cannot rely on being able to combine public criticism with continued access.

Likewise, our China researcher believes that her description of the Chinese political system as 'fragmented' might not please the government, but since it does not aim to undermine the Chinese Communist Party, she does not believe she would really be denied access to her home country. Again, the relative obscurity of academic work also makes a difference:

journalists from the west are much more regularly denied access than scholars. This difference seems to be confirmed by the recent experience of a colleague in China, who was recently 'invited for a cup of tea' by security agents because of (English-language) news coverage of an academic publication of hers.

Our Iran researcher by contrast has, in the very specific context of the repressive aftermath of the 2009 election protests, initiated an activist-oriented edited volume (Michaelsen 2011) that he thought could compromise future access. He found the situation in Iran so dramatic at that time that he wanted to take a position. He decided that the story told by this book, edited together with 11 journalists who left the country and wrote about their experiences during and after the protests, was more important than going back to Iran. The book was published in English and Farsi, and he gave interviews about it to Farsi language online media in the diaspora considered inimical by the regime. When, six years later, he prepared for another trip to Iran, he did briefly wonder whether this publication might compromise his access to and security in the field, but he still thinks that there are times when academic researchers should take a clear and principled position.

Another way of disseminating our work, perhaps the most effective way in numerical terms, is by acting as commentators in western media. The increasing emphasis on societal engagement, moreover, may propel scholars to think that all publicity is good publicity. We do sometimes give radio interviews, or allow ourselves to be quoted in newspapers, but we are very careful about the exact wording. In case of print media, we always insist on seeing and being allowed to correct quotes before publication. A more negative phrasing than we are comfortable with, sometimes desired by journalists, not only interferes with the nuance of what we want to say, it can also have consequences for our access to the country and to sources in the country.

A final consideration, when it comes to weighing publicity against future access, is the extent to which our careers and our lives are bound up with one country and its political system. Our India and Mexico researcher and our Malaysia researcher have not been much concerned about future access to the relevant countries, in part because such denial of access is relatively rare, but primarily because, at this point in their career at least, they are mixed-methods researchers who think of themselves as political scientists who happened to do fieldwork in one or two specific countries. Our Morocco researcher found doing research in Tunisia to make a refreshing change and is also thinking about broadening her expertise to

West Africa. Our Kazakhstan researcher thinks of herself as a country expert first and foremost, but has also written on Central Asia more generally, and considers future research on Russia. Our Iran researcher, while he has invested profoundly in learning Farsi and understanding Iran, has partly shifted his research agenda, toward studying the Iranian diaspora, on the one hand, and a broader comparative focus on media in authoritarian contexts on the other hand. While the primary motivation for broadening our research agendas has not been to mitigate against the risk of the authoritarian state obstructing our research, it does make it easier to navigate the dilemmas regarding publicity and access. Our China researcher is more exclusively invested in understanding the universe that is China, albeit comparatively. Moreover, she is and wants to remain a Chinese citizen, so for her the stakes in navigating what to write, and where to write it, are higher, as they are likely to be for any national investigating their own country. In sum, we all think of how we couch our criticisms of authoritarian regimes and how publicly we do so, in relation to future access as a trade-off, but the choices we make depend on our specific professional and personal relation to the field.

Chapter Conclusion: Shifting the Transparency Debate

There is an inherent tension in doing, but especially in publishing, research on authoritarianism. Ahram and Goode (2016, 838) describe authoritarian regimes as 'engines of agnotology', by which they mean that these regimes have an interest in maintaining ignorance and uncertainty about many aspects of how they function. Hence, publication can raise problems for our future access, but more importantly, potential harm to sources. We add our voice to the chorus of scholars who have argued that a concern for transparency in research cannot be translated into a requirement to make transcripts or field notes public, even in anonymized version. Nor should they be stored in potentially unsafe digital repositories. Our responsibility to do no harm to respondents is simply paramount. But we have also tried to go beyond only rejecting inappropriate transparency requirements. In this chapter and in this book, we have tried to increase transparency about *how* we do research: by explaining in detail how we have navigated the methodological and ethical trade-offs that follow from doing research in the authoritarian field, and what general learnings we think may be gleaned from our common experiences.

References

Ahram, A. I., & Goode, J. P. (2016). Researching Authoritarianism in the Discipline of Democracy. *Social Science Quarterly, 97*(2016), 834–849. https://doi.org/10.1111/ssqu.12340.

Art, D. (2016). Archivists and Adventurers: Research Strategies for Authoritarian Regimes of the Past and Present. *Social Science Quarterly, 97*, 974–990. https://doi.org/10.1111/ssqu.12348.

Bellin, E. (2016). Comment on (April 06, 2.03): "Risks and Practices to Avoid?" in *IV.1. Authoritarian/Repressive Political Regimes*. Retrieved July 20, 2017, from https://www.qualtd.net/viewtopic.php?f=26&t=174#p640.

Del Sordi, A. (2016). Legitimation and the Party of Power in Kazakhstan. In M. Brusis, J. Ahrens, & M. S. Wessel (Eds.), *Politics and Legitimacy in Post-Soviet Eurasia* (pp. 72–96). London: Palgrave Macmillan.

Directorate-General Research & Innovation. (2016). *Open Innovation, Open Science, Open to the World*. European Commission. Retrieved from https://publications.europa.eu/en/publication-detail/-/publication/3213b335-1cbc-11e6-ba9a-01aa75ed71a1.

Driscoll, J. (2015). Can Anonymity Promises Possibly Be Credible in Police States? In M. Golder & S. N. Golder (Eds.), *Comparative Politics Newsletter. Comparative Politics of the American Political Science Association, 25*, 4–7.

Joint Position Paper. (2017). Joint Position Paper on the European Open Science Cloud. *Open Science, Germany and The Netherlands*. Retrieved July 23, 2017, from https://www.openscience.nl/binaries/content/assets/subsites-evenementen/open-science/joint-position-paper-on-the-european-open-science-cloud-de-nl.pdf.

Loyle, C. E. (2016). Overcoming Research Obstacles in Hybrid Regimes: Lessons from Rwanda. *Social Science Quarterly, 97*(4), 923–935.

Lynch, M. (2016). Area Studies and the Cost of Prematurely Implementing DA-RT. In M. Golder & Soma N. Golder (Eds.), *Comparative Politics Newsletter. Comparative Politics of the American Political Science Association, 26*, 36–40.

March for Science. (2017). *Principles and Goals*. Retrieved July 20, 2017, from https://www.marchforscience.com/mission-and-vision/.

Michaelsen, M. (2011). *Election Fallout. Iran's Exiled Journalists on Their Struggle for Democratic Change*. Berlin: Hans Schiler Verlag. Open Access under: http://library.fes.de/pdf-files/iez/08560.pdf.

Pew Center. (2017). *U.S. Public Trust in Science* (Rainie, L.). Retrieved July 20, 2017, from http://www.pewinternet.org/2017/06/27/u-s-public-trust-in-science-and-scientists/.

Shih, V. (2015). Research in Authoritarian Regimes: Transparency Tradeoffs and Solutions. In T. Buthe & A. M. Jacobs (Eds.), *Qualitative and Multi-Method Research. American Political Science Association, 13*, 20–22.

Stroschein, S. (2016). Comment on: (April 23, 4:48 am): "Danger, Harm and Change" in *IV.1. Authoritarian/Repressive Political Regimes.* Retrieved July 20, 2017, from https://www.qualtd.net/viewtopic.php?f=26&t=174#p640.

Tripp, A. (2016). Comment on (April 13, 7:26 am): "Privileging Quantitative Methods and Challenging Field Work Condition" in *IV.1. Authoritarian/Repressive Political Regimes.* Retrieved July 20, 2017, from https://www.qualtd.net/viewtopic.php?f=26&t=174#p640.

Dos and Don'ts in the Authoritarian Field

Chapter 1 Introduction

- Do not take any of our recommendations below as Gospel. Every context, every individual situation is different. Consult others, but use your own judgment.
- Do engage in authoritarian fieldwork. It is not always easy, but it is much needed, and ultimately rewarding.

Chapter 2 Entering the Field

- Do take ethics procedures seriously, and fight for appropriate ethics procedures at your home institution if they are either unhelpfully rigid, or non-existent.
- Prepare by reading human rights reports and embassy briefs, but be aware of their biases, and triangulate. Consult academics and others who often go to your field.
- Don't act like a spy. Be open about being a social science researcher on a fieldwork trip. Carry official letters from your university and business cards.
- Practice digital security routines before leaving, but abandon them in the field where appropriate.
- Take it slow, especially on a first visit, or when the political situation has evolved, or when you have a new, more sensitive topic. Be patient; acclimatize to the local politics.

M. Glasius et al., *Research, Ethics and Risk in the Authoritarian Field*,
https://doi.org/10.1007/978-3-319-68966-1

- You will have preconceptions, but remain willing to revise them when faced with surprises. Be critical but not judgmental.
- Be prepared to encounter security agents and answer questions, but don't get obsessed with this risk.
- Think of digital security measures in terms of trade-offs: between greater digital security on the one hand and data loss, arousing suspicion, or getting paranoid on the other hand.

Chapter 3 Learning the Red Lines

- Get acquainted with the 'hard red lines', that is, political taboo topics, of your field before you leave. Stay away from them unless you are an experienced researcher.
- Make it boring (Malekzadeh 2016, 865). Do not tell lies about your research, but present it in ways that are neutral, non-specific, and depoliticized.
- Get locals to vet your wording, so interview or survey questions sound harmless enough but still elicit meaningful responses.
- Think through whether you need to adapt your behavior to stay within the red lines—but don't get paranoid.
- Red lines may shift, so what you thought you knew may no longer apply. Be prepared to adapt if words and behaviors previously acceptable turn out to be taboo or vice versa.

Chapter 4 Building and Maintaining Relations in the Field

- Invest time and effort in building a network, so you come to interviewees ('respondents') with a recommendation.
- When working with local collaborators, consider the potentially greater risks they may run, and their possible dependence on you, before making requests.
- Be patient but persistent when trying to get interviews.
- Give potential respondents every reason to trust you, by being professional, respectful, reliable, accessible, and discreet.
- Meet in places that are considered culturally and politically appropriate to the context and will make both you and your respondent feel most comfortable.

- When meeting respondents, do not get straight to the point: make small-talk, start with innocuous questions, work your way up to the more sensitive ones.
- Be aware of, and work with, your ascriptive characteristics (age, gender, national background), your personality, and a respondent's likely preconceptions, as best as you can to establish a relationship and elicit information.
- Approach respondents with respect, not confrontation (even if they are themselves antagonistic). Treat their perspective as intrinsically interesting as well as in need of triangulation and critical analysis.
- Acknowledge that collaborators and respondents are giving you their time and confidence, and think through what you can do in return, without giving offense or posing ethical problems.

Chapter 5 Mental Impact

- Do not be ashamed of being afraid: when doing research in the authoritarian field, you may sometimes feel anxious, afraid, even a little paranoid.
- Talk openly about your difficulties in getting access to data in the field, and you will find them to be widespread.
- Do talk about stressful incidents, hard stories or traumatic events, and the impact they are having on how you feel, with trusted locals as well as with friends and colleagues, during and after fieldwork.
- Recognize symptoms of stress, anxiety, and possible traumatization; take steps to mitigate these feelings, but accept that you may need the safety of home, and the distance in time and space, to fully evaluate and deal with them.
- Do not neglect your body: the combined physical impact of pollution, temperature changes, change of diet, and hard work can compound negative mental impact.
- Do not seek out situations likely to cause trauma: neither data-gathering for the sake of a career nor the desire to give voice to victims is worth knowingly incurring post-traumatic stress.
- When coming back from fieldwork involving stressful incidents, hard stories, or traumatic events, consider debriefing, professional counseling, or spiritual (self-)help, whatever works for you.

- Reflect on how stressful incidents, hard stories, or traumatic events affect your written work, considering the possible validity gain, but also the risk of bias or self-censorship.
- Do not be deterred: authoritarian field research is inspiring.

Chapter 6 Writing It Up

- Do not put respondents at risk for the sake of transparency.
- Consider what kinds of respondents you are interviewing, and think through what that should entail for whether and if so how to anonymize.
- Consult with respondents on exactly whether and if so how they can or cannot be cited—but anonymize even despite their permission when you think naming puts them at risk.
- Consider everything anonymization entails: omitting other identifying features, keeping contact details separate from transcripts, taking digital security measures when appropriate
- Consider sharing anonymized transcripts with close colleagues and with editors on request.
- In publications, justify why it is necessary to anonymize, and make clear why the anonymous respondents are relevant sources of information.
- In publications, be as transparent as possible about your practices: how you came by respondents, limitations and biases, the kinds of questions asked, informed consent-related conversations, taped or written records, how you stored them during and after fieldwork, and so on.
- Reflect on the consequences of storing transcripts and other materials in digital repositories for respondent risk.
- Beyond academic publications, consider the trade-off between public criticism of the authoritarian regime and future access in relation to your own investment in the field.

Do not take any of our recommendations above as Gospel. Every context, every individual situation is different. Consult others, but use your own judgment

www.ingramcontent.com/pod-product-compliance
Lightning Source LLC
LaVergne TN
LVHW082238200926
848484LV00008B/2371
* 9 7 8 1 0 1 3 2 9 0 8 3 1 *